The
Philosopher's
Tool Kit

The
Philosopher's
Tool Kit

Steven Scott Aspenson

M.E. Sharpe

Armonk, New York
London, England

Library of Congress Cataloging-in-Publication Data

Aspenson, Steven Scott, 1961-
The philosopher's tool kit / Steven Scott Aspenson.
p. cm.
Includes bibliographical references and index.
ISBN 0-7656-0217-2 (alk. paper). — ISBN 07656-0218-0 (pbk. : alk. paper)
1. Philosophy—Introductions. I. Title.
BD21.A86 1997
101—DC21 97-16070
CIP
Printed in the United States of America

The paper used in this publication meets the minimum requirements of
American National Standard for Information Sciences—
Permanence of Paper for Printed Library Materials,
ANSI Z 39.48-1984.

MV (c)   10   9   8   7   6   5   4   3   2   1
MV (p)   10   9   8   7   6   5   4   3   2   1

For my lovely wife, Caroline

Contents

Preface

I intend that this book supplement philosophy course work at both the undergraduate and graduate levels. During my graduate studies it was a frustration to me that philosophy's conceptual mainstays, the notions of substance, internal and external relation, category, definition, *a priori* knowledge, principle, axiom, and so on, were nowhere collected together and explained in a single work—and discussion of those notions with faculty and other graduate students usually left me worrying that something had been left out. This book is my effort at a remedy.

Dictionaries and glossaries of introductory texts often provide difficult or misleading definitions by failing to provide a useful context. Recent philosophy of language suggests that this shortcoming, the failure to provide context for philosophy's *conventional* notions, may render even accurate definitions useless for grasping the meanings of terms. It also makes the definitions difficult to remember. I have tried to improve on dictionaries in two ways: first, I provide the required context *by chapter,* which provides perspective and a framework for understanding, and second, I provide *illustrative* definitions.

I have also tried to strike a balance between accuracy and clarity. An accurate rendering of a notion often presupposes a rather large understanding of context, and so is unclear; a rendering that is clear to the student is often misleading. While I do not think this book will make philosophy easy for beginners, I do think it will make misunderstanding much easier to avoid.

Acknowledgments

I want to acknowledge my debt to an excellent philosopher, Eric Hockett, foremost, for his many insightful comments on drafts of this book. And to Professor Richard Fumerton, at the University of Iowa, who helped me avoid a number of errors in chapter 3. Actually, it was Richard's example that inspired this book in the first place. When I began studying, he was choosing up teams for a football game on Union Field, dividing us into Theists and Atheists. Spinning the ball, he asked me, "are you a theist or an atheist?" Not to give myself away, I said, "I'm not sure." He responded, "Well, do you think there are universals?" I squinted at him and said yes. "You're a theist," he said, "get over there."

It struck me then, and I learned it was common praise among the other graduate students, that Richard had a particularly refined flowchart of principles in his mind that allowed him to tell where a view would go, given certain fundamental commitments. Writing this book began as an effort to acquire that same virtue.

I would be remiss, in this context, not to mention Professor Ron Glass, at the University of Wisconsin–La Crosse, who, with a similar virtue, helped me with practically every important philosophical view I've tried to develop. I can only guess what sort of sad understanding of philosophy I'd have without his help.

Finally, I want to thank Professor Tom Sullivan, at the University of St. Thomas, St. Paul, for his scholarly comments on the first chapter. His comments remind me that, in my effort not to write beyond my skill, I have not pursued every piece of advice from any of the contributors mentioned here, and wish to convey to the reader that any inaccuracies, I am certain, are due to my own failings.

Introduction

There has been a slow and sporadic increase and refinement in the philosopher's conceptual resources throughout the history of philosophy. Characterized as an *a priori* discipline, philosophy makes its progress by employing what now have become tried-and-true tools of thought, tools of the trade if you will. This book is an effort, in a short space, to introduce those tools and illustrate their common uses. Supplying an exhaustive account of the tools philosophers have employed to date would be an ambitious and perhaps unnecessary effort; but rendering the most popular and practical of those tools accessible to beginning and intermediate students of philosophy would not.

What follows is something like a lab manual used in a natural science course. But while lab manuals teach students to use tools prebuilt and waiting in the laboratory (Bunsen burners, petri dishes, star globes, and so on), this manual requires that students make their own tools. Not to worry, constructing those tools requires no preexisting material beyond an attentive mind and experience of the world common to most of us at about age five.

I should say just a few words about philosophy in general. Philosophers have found that efforts to advance knowledge about reality sort naturally into two very general kinds of studies—the two most noteworthy areas of philosophy. The first, sometimes called "first philosophy," is Metaphysics—the study of the basic nature of reality. And, as one might expect, stubborn questions about reality naturally lead to the second study, Epistemology—the exploration of our abilities to know various things or to arrive at justified beliefs about them.

Understanding and using the tools presented in this book requires some context. Familiarity with the enduring themes of philosophy is crucial for beginning students of philosophy to grasp fully the technical terms and other devices that make up the tools philosophers employ. The following chapters, then, are interwoven to form a sketch of current academic philosophical enterprise. Chapter 1 focuses on metaphysics and the tools philosophers rely on most frequently in clarifying its issues and in attempting to identify and solve its problems. Chapters 2 and 3 focus on epistemological tools, chapter 4 on tools of philosophical analysis, and the last chapter on tools related to philosophical writing.

You will find a list of *related terms* at the end of each chapter. Think of these terms not as mere added detail but as the notions that are the focus of the book, the tools—conceptual devices—to be mastered. Think of the subject matter of the chapter as introducing a framework of concepts that forms the basic context trained philosophers rely on when thinking about particular philosophical issues—a context that allows for getting one's bearings in the muddle of philosophical terminology. Where it is useful for under-standing a given topic, I allude to or comment on philosophical issues, sometimes using terms explained elsewhere in the book. Throughout you will also find notes to readings, both to original texts and to helpful secondary sources.

The
Philosopher's
Tool Kit

Chapter 1

Categories, Classification, and Definition

1.0 Introduction

Modeled on the work of the great Greek philosopher Aristotle, the present chapter sketches a map philosophers have used to orient themselves around the enterprise of metaphysics for the past 2,300 years. Paying close attention to the highlighted words and carefully studying the related terms at the end of the chapter will pay great dividends when approaching the formidable task of understanding original texts, or in merely following what is going on in classroom discussions of philosophical issues.

The following three sections introduce a web of organizational concepts. Study them together as a unit. Keep in mind that many interesting details are left out in the interest of saving space. Those details should, however, be easy to add as the basics below become familiar.

1.1 Categories

Systematically, perhaps the best first step to take in beginning to study the basic nature of reality is the step to organize it. Linguists have noted that no matter where one travels in the world, descriptive statements in all languages seem to share the subject/predicate form of our own. That, a professor of mine mused, is probably because no matter where one travels in the world, there will always be *things* and something to say *about them*. That is, reality, as it is naturally conceptualized, comes in two very general kinds of entities: *things* and their *features*. Aristotle, the first really great organizer, thought of the first of those kinds of entities as belonging to the category of **Substance** (see section 1.4). The features of substances he found he could divide into nine further categories: quality, quantity, relation, place, time, position, possessing, acting and being acted upon. All ten of Aristotle's categories are listed horizontally in Figure 1.1 on page 6 with concrete examples of the kinds of entities that fall into each category.[1]

These categories, Aristotle apparently thinks, divide the world at the joints.[2] That is, they name *real kinds* of entities and features of the world; they are not merely arbitrary and changeable ways of sorting things, as are the ways we organize our closets or dresser drawers.

Much of Aristotle's *Categories* is devoted to setting out his views about the natures of the things in the categories, as well as about various relations that hold among those things. For example, substances are the only things that are *independent* of other things for their existence. Unlike a quality (like a particular instance of red), a substance can exist without "piggy-backing" on something else. Red cannot exist by itself—just floating around somewhere. It must be *tied* to a substance that *is* red (see **Relation: Exemplification** in section 1.4). A relation such as 'being taller than' cannot exist apart from its *relata*—the substances that stand in that relation, for example, Goliath to Napoleon. But this is to get into details of Aristotle's metaphysics rather than merely to orient ourselves to that general discipline. Let's proceed to classification.

1.2 Classification

Classifications, listed vertically in the expanded chart opposite, show increasing degrees of **abstraction** (see section 4.3) as one reads *up* from the particular entities that fall into each of the categories. For illustrative purposes I have chosen what is already, I hope, a familiar classification schema: Kingdom, Phylum, Class, Order, Family, Genus, and Species.[3] Classification terms such as these should be thought of as *contrasting* with category terms—the categories *do not* sort things according to varying degrees of abstraction; one should think of the categories as *ultimate* genera, or ultimately abstract genera. (See Figure 1.2, page 6).

The use of classification terms can be confusing. You will often see the terms 'genus' and 'species' applied to the same thing (or class) depending on what the thing (or class) is being referred to. To take an example from geometry: the class of triangles might be called a *genus* (general term) in

Substance	Quality	Quantity	Relation	Place	Time	Position	Possessing	Acting	Being Acted Upon
SOCRATES	WHITE	ONE	FRIEND OF PLATO	IN ATHENS	400 B.C.	SITTING	HAVING A TOGA	SPEAKING	BEING SPOKEN TO

Figure 1.1. **Aristotle's categories with examples**

Substance	Quality	Quantity	Relation	Place	Time	Position	Possessing	Acting	Being Acted Upon
Kingdom									
Phylum									
Class									
Order									
Family									
Genus									
Species									
SOCRATES	WHITE	ONE	FRIEND OF PLATO	IN ATHENS	400 B.C.	SITTING	HAVING A TOGA	SPEAKING	BEING SPOKEN TO

Figure 1.2. **Categories with classification examples**

reference to particular triangles like isosceles, right, equilateral, and so on.

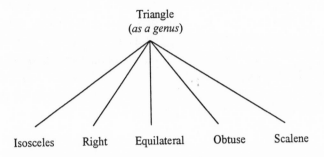

On the other hand, that same class of triangles might be called a *species* (specific term) in reference to some more general classification, for example, the class of plane figures.

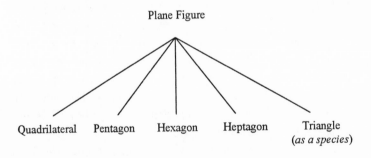

So the same class may, relatively, be either a genus or a species. You will also see in philosophical literature that, instead of using 'family' for a genus that has two levels of specification below it, that genus may be called a *remote* (far) genus and the level immediately collective of the species the *proximate* (near) genus—it is only in comprehensive efforts to classify a given subject matter that rigid designations such as those of biologists mentioned above are used.

A noteworthy feature of the genus-species relation is that whatever is true of a given genus is true of its species, though not vice versa. If an animal is capable of self-motion, then humans, dogs, aardvarks, and so forth, are so capable. Knowledge of animal nature entails knowledge of all the various species of animals *insofar as they are animals.*

1.3 Definition

If you look at the even more expanded chart below, you will see the term 'differentia' written conspicuously off to the side of the classification terms. I have done this because the feature (of a thing or class) referred to as a 'difference' plays a special role in classification, the role of *defining* the thing or class. It is in virtue of the *difference* that species are differentiated from each other under some genus. The classic example, from Aristotle throughout the Middle Ages, is that the difference *rational* differentiates one kind of animal from all others. That is, rational is the defining feature of humans under the genus animal. Humans are rational animals. That is their definition. 'Rational' is the differentia that defines an animal as a human animal.

Below, I illustrate the role of differentia in classification using a standard biological example. Hominids are biologically differentiated from other primates according to their bipedalism and erect bone structure. A biologist's definition of 'Hominid' then might be 'bipedal primate'.

Definition, in the sense above, is to be distinguished from verbal definition. Verbal definitions are found in dic-

Substance

Animalia
Chordata
Mammalia
Primates   Bipedalism (Differentia)
Hominidae
Homo

Sapiens

SOCRATES

tionaries—the definitions of words. Aristotle's definitions are *real* definitions—the definitions of *things* in the world rather than words, and are intended to express the **essence** (see section 1.4) or *whatness* of those things. They are intended to tell us what something *is* as opposed to telling us what some word *means,* and as opposed to telling us *whether* or *that* something is (whether or that something exists)—a matter perhaps our own senses or the testimony of others must inform us about.

There are, as one might expect, other philosophical views about the nature of definition.[4] There are other accounts of the content and structure of the world that avoid the hotly disputed category of substance altogether.[5] But the above three sections provide an essential starting point for understanding the very common terms philosophers use to talk about and orient themselves around the subject matter of metaphysics.

The importance of this section for grasping a view of philosophy that still affects how things are understood today cannot be overemphasized. Aristotle's system of categories, classification, and definition does not merely provide us with a means of seeing how the world is arranged. It illustrates an indispensable kind of framework theoretical *understanding* depends on—whether one thinks that framework should be Aristotle's, that of modern science, or yet some other.[6]

Studying the above sort of organizational system results in acquiring groups of mutually complementary concepts. Such study supposes that one understands individual things in a certain powerful and comprehensive way by understanding their placement in the system—the system of categories, classification, and definition. Some medieval and ancient philosophers thought that knowing something was to know its definition, its real definition, and of course, that meant knowing its genus, its species, and its differentia. Now, to understand the proximate genus, in the above definition of Hominid, is, in part, to understand that of which it is a species (if it is a species of some other genus, i.e., not an ultimate genus), and so deeper understanding of a thing supposes that one understands the remote genus as well. Carried on, it may be that a complete understanding of something supposes that one understands *all* the remote genera. Further, *completely* understanding the category within which the definition falls may presuppose understanding of its relations to the other categories.

1.4 Essential Terms of Metaphysics

Accident (cf. **Proprium** below): any feature of a thing that it may have at one time and lack at another and still remain the same thing.[7] 'Being pale' may belong to a person before a joke and not to them afterward; or it may belong to them before going to the beach and later not. Any item falling under nine of the ten categories (excluding Substance) can be an accident only if it is not an essential property (see **Property: Essential** below).

Accidental Form (see **Form** below).

Cause: Aristotle distinguishes four different kinds of causation: Efficient, Material, Final, and Formal. Consider Aristotle's example of the causes of a statue: the sculptor is the *efficient cause,* that which produces the statue; the bronze or marble is the *material cause* (see **Matter** below), that of which the statue is made; the finished statue is the *final cause,* the end for which the sculpturing was done; and the shape, color, density, and so on, constitute the *formal cause* (see **Form** below), that which provides for what the thing is.

Contemporary discussions of causation are limited almost exclusively to the nature of efficient causation, in large part due to David Hume's critique of the notion. Efficient causation is interesting to philosophers because it seems a cause and its characteristic effect are logically distinct (see **Logical Relation** in section 3.4), that is, there is no conceptually *necessary* connection between cause and effect. Some interesting questions, then, are: What sort of necessity might there be between an efficient cause and its effect? Is there any sense of 'necessary' that is legitimate in regard to events? What happens to inquiry and experimentation in science if cause and effect are linked necessarily?

Continuant: a kind of entity that can exist over time. Contrasted with momentary particulars, a continuant is not extinguished by the passage of time.

Determinable/Determinate: a type of classification similar to Genus/Species classification, respectively (see sections 1.2 and 1.3 above). A determinable such as color has as its determinates red, blue, green, and so on. Determinates differ from species in that they are not differentiated by a differentia. There is no differentia of red under 'color' to distinguish it from blue. Red and blue seemingly share nothing except what belongs to them *qua* colors, yet are not the same. And since varying species are distinguished under some genus in virtue of their differentia, new terminology to reflect that difference was coined.[8]

Essence (Latin: *Quiddity,* whatness): usually contrasted with existence, an essence or *nature* is *what*ever any particular thing is. A horse, a cow, a dog all share existence equally, but they all differ in that they have different essences: horseness, cowness, and dogness, respectively. Horseness is the abstract whatness of a particular horse that may have, on some philosophical views, an individual whatness called, for example, 'Triggerness' or 'Mr. Edness'.

Form (cf. **Matter** and **Substance** below): in Aristotelian and medieval metaphysics individual substances are composites of matter and form (some medievals thought that even spiritual substances, like angelic souls, were composites of spiritual matter and form). The formal aspect of a form-matter composite may be either a *substantial form* or an *accidental form*.[9] Substantial form accounts for what kind of thing a particular substance is: the substantial form of water is what makes a given parcel of matter water, rather than something else. If there is no substantial form of ice—and ice is merely a change in water that does not change what it is—then ice is an accidental form (see **Accident** above). I say "*if* there is no substantial form of ice" because various philosophers differ about what substantial forms there are in nature. This last point suggests a distinction between *natural* and *artificial* (from artifact) substantial forms. Thomas Aquinas, for example, thinks bread is an artificial form, but a genuine substantial form nonetheless.[10]

Identity (cf. **Identity Statement** in section 2.3): sometimes called a reflexive relation (a relation whose terms or relata are only one thing), the identity of a thing is the property or relation of 'being the same as itself'. Since everything is the same as itself, some think identity is a transcendental property (see **Transcendental** below).

Individuation (cf. **Universal** and **Matter** below): an abstract verb referring to the 'act' of individuating, or the abstract noun referring to the topic of what individuates. For example, what provides the individuality of two qualitatively identical red spots, or the individuality of two instances of circularity? Is it Matter? Spatial location? Existence?[11]

Intentionality: the precise **abstraction** (see section 4.3) of a characteristic of consciousness: that consciousness is *al-*

ways consciousness of something. 'Intentionality' refers to the *aboutness* of thought—its *directedness* to an object.

Those philosophers who think that the mind is nothing but the brain have as a central goal an eliminatively reductive explanation of intentionality (see **Reduction** in section 4.3). That is, they must explain away this apparent fact of immediate experience, perhaps in an account of how material objects can be *about* or *of* other material objects in the required sense, or in an account of how intentionality is illusory.

Matter (cf. **Substance** below, and **Form** above): crudely, the 'stuff' of substances (material and, on some views, spiritual substances). Matter, as understood by Aristotle, cannot exist without Form, and is what accounts for the individuality (see **Individuation** above) of general things like flesh and bone: it is what makes flesh and bone *this* flesh and *these* bones.

In some Metaphysical theories, matter is seemingly posited to explain the possibility of *substantial change* (change from one kind of thing into another different kind of thing, rather than a simple change of a single substance, for example, when a car becomes dented it changes but remains the same kind of thing). For example, if earth, air, fire, and water were the fundamental elements of physical reality, as thought in ancient and medieval views of the world, and water could change into air, one way of explaining the change would be to say that while the substantial form of water disappeared and the substantial form of air came to be, there would be a *change* of water to air only if there was something in *common* to the two quantities of water and air. That common thing would be matter, and would account for the event being a *change* of one into the other, instead of being a miraculous replacement of one for the other.[12]

Necessity/Contingency (see section 2.3).

Ontology: lit., the study of being or existence. Often, an 'ontology' is a list of what kinds of things exist. A sophisticated ontology may try to distinguish different kinds or modes of existence. For example, it may include a distinction between things with 'full-blown' existence (perhaps the tree in the backyard) as opposed to things merely having 'being' (perhaps a unicorn). Some even think that an ontology ought to admit of things that do not exist at all, yet are part of reality: Alexius Meinong thinks there are nonexistent objects: the unicorn mentioned above would be an example.[13] An ontology may also distinguish the *manner* in which things exist—existence dependent on or independent of something else, necessary and contingent existence, potential and actual existence, and so forth.

Organic Unity (cf. **Supervenience** and **Organic Whole** below): the valuational metaphysical notion of a unity of elements with a resulting value that is not reducible to the additive values of those elements. For example, the value of awareness added to the value of beauty may be less than the value of awareness-of-beauty.

Organic Whole (cf. **Organic Unity** above): the notion of organism at work in this common term calls attention to the relation the parts of an organism have to each other and to the organism itself. According to G.E. Moore, calling something an organic whole is either to call attention to the notion that the parts of an organism have "no meaning or significance apart from the whole" or that the parts are related to each other and the whole as means to ends.[14]

Particular (cf. **Universal** below): an individual existing thing, either a substance or an *instance* of an accident or property. Not a 'general' entity, but a concrete example of a kind: this blue, that square, these sounds, as opposed to blueness, squareness, and sound in general. Particulars need not be material or physical items: if there are souls, each soul will be a particular, though nonmaterial, entity.

Possibility/Impossibility (see section 2.3).

Predicable: any term that may be *truly* joined to the grammatical subject of a sentence with some form of the verb 'to be' is a predicable. There are four important 'ises' philosophers commonly distinguish:

(1) The 'is' of predication.
(2) The 'is' of existence.
(3) The 'is' of identity.
(4) The 'is' of definition.

Regarding (1), the five most general kinds of predicate terms are: Genus: Socrates is *an animal;* Species: Socrates is *a man;* Difference: Socrates is *rational;* Property: Aristotle is *the father of Nicomachus* or *the tutor of Alexander the Great;* and Accident: Plato is *white* or *a friend of Socrates.*

Of these five, Aristotle distinguishes those that are 'said of' a subject or 'present in' a subject. The *said of* predicates appear to be those that are either classificatory of or are otherwise external to the subject: Genus, Species, and Difference terms are classificatory as they are qualifications of things by *abstraction* (see **Abstraction** in section 4.3). Various Properties and Accidents are external to their subjects: being under the roof, being supine, being spoken to, and so on. The *present in* predicates appear to be those that are exemplified (see **Relation: Exemplification** below) by the subject. Various Properties and Accidents are 'in' their subjects: being white, being aware of something, being warm, and so on.[15]

Regarding (2), the term 'is' can itself be a predicate, along with its conjugates: I am; We are; The chair is; meaning, I exist; We exist, The chair exists.

Regarding (3), see **Identity** above, and especially, **Identity Statement** in section 2.3.

Regarding (4), the term 'is' can mean 'definitionally equivalent to'. This sense of 'is' must be distinguished from the 'is' of predication, though, on occasion, it might appear to be merely a species of classificatory predicates from (1) above. That is, the sentence "Man is a rational animal" might appear to be just a complex case of a *said of* predicate. But there is more going on since the grammatical predicate is defining, or expressing the essence of, the subject. Note also that there is a close relation between the *is* of definition and the *is* of identity. What is the difference between an identity statement and a definition? (See section 1.3.)

Proper Part: a part of a complex object that can exist

independently of other parts of that object, or of the object itself. The surface of a table, though a part of the table, is not a proper part, since it cannot exist apart from the table. A leg of the table, in contrast, can exist apart from the table, and so is a proper part.

Property: although common philosophical usage employs the term 'property' to mean almost any feature of a thing (as I will use it in this book on occasion) Aristotle defines a property as a feature of a thing or kind of thing that is *unique* to that thing or kind. For example, if a proton is the only kind of substance with a positive charge, the feature 'having a positive charge' is a property of a proton. Since both a proton and a neutron partially compose an atom, the feature 'partially composes an atom' is *not* a property of a proton but merely an accidental feature of it.

Aristotle distinguishes two further kinds of properties: **relative properties** and **temporary properties.** An example of the first would be a feature unique to something as it is compared with something else—if you were the only person *in the group* with blond hair, the feature 'has blond hair' would be a relative property of you since it is unique to you relative to the others in the group. It would *not,* of course, be a property of you *sans phrase.* An example of the second kind would be a feature unique to something at a particular time—if you are the only person in the universe coughing at midnight, December 31, 1999, the feature 'coughing' will be a temporary property of you.

Compositive Property (cf. **Divisive Property** below): any property that, if it is a property of the proper parts of a thing, is also a property of the whole thing. 'Being green' is a compositive property, since anything made up of green proper parts is itself green. 'Weighing five pounds' is not a compositive property, since anything composed of parts weighing five pounds does not weigh five pounds. Being magnetized, being extended, being heavy, and being warm are all compositive properties.[16]

Conjunctive Property: a property whose elements are conjoined. If the world contained only people who were either tall and fat or short and thin, then 'being tall' *would not* be a property of Michael Jordan, and 'being thin' *would not* be a property of him, but 'being tall and thin' *would* be a property of him.

Disjunctive Property: a property whose elements are disjoined. For example, the property of being 'greater than or equal to or less than', or as it might be seen, '$\geq\leq$', is a disjunctive property. Properties of such a property are transitivity, reflexivity, and symmetry. A disjunctive property might be thought to be the reference of the determinable 'color'. Should we understand 'color' as referring to the disjunctive property of being red, or green, or yellow, or blue, or brown, and so on? Philosophers who reject the existence of abstract objects like color, and suggest such a disjunctive property as an eliminatively reductive analysis (see **Reduction,** section 4.3), must answer the question, How do we know what to list under the term 'color'? Doesn't our ability to use the term color without knowing anything like the entire list of particular colors tell against such a reduction?

19

Divisive Property (cf. **Compositive Property** above): any property that, if it is a property of some compound thing, is also a property of some proper part of that thing. 'Being extended' is a divisive property, since any compound thing that is extended also has a proper part that is extended. 'Being heavy' is not a divisive property, since a compound thing that is heavy need not, because of that, have parts that are heavy.

Essential Property: a constitutive property of a thing—a property that, if lacking, destroys the identity of the thing (or destroys what, and thereby that, the thing is). For example, 'rationality', if it is lacking from a person, destroys the person (or the personhood of a person). An animal of some other kind than human results. ('Rational' meaning 'capable of reasoning'—in contrast not to irrational but to *nonrational*.)

Intrinsic Property (see **Monadic Property** below).

Monadic Property (from Latin: *Monad,* meaning unit or one): also known as an 'intrinsic property', a monadic property is a *nonrelational* property of a thing. Having a positive charge is a monadic property of a proton because the positive charge and the proton form a unit that is not naturally thought of as a relation. We might say that protons *exemplify* a positive charge (see **Relation: Exemplification** below). Partially composing an atom is a nonmonadic or *relational* property of a proton because that property depends on some other thing than the proton (i.e., the rest of the atom).

Relative Property (see **Property** above).

Second-Order Property (Feature) (cf. **Supervenience** below): a property of a property (or a feature of a feature). The quality of being bright is a quality of some colors, say yellow. The relation of being 'second-order' is that of being a feature of the same kind of feature—a desire for a desire, a universal of a universal, a claim about a claim.

Temporary Property: (see **Property** above).

Proprium: a proprium is a necessary accident (see **Accident** above). Medievals coined the term to pick out those features of a thing which, although they do not enter into its definition, seem to follow necessarily from some defining feature. The classic example, 'risibility', the capacity for laughter, is a proprium of humans, since it follows necessarily from being rational, the defining feature of the humans.

Relation (Internal/External): an internal relation is one that is necessary and unchanging *because of intrinsic features (nonrelational features)* of the relata. The relation of 'being darker than' is an internal relation between blue and yellow because of the intrinsic characters of the colors blue and yellow. But 'being darker than' can be an external relation, for example, between my coat and my hat. That relation, depending on what colors they happen to be (imagine they are both blue), is not necessary and can change for many and varied reasons, for example, if the darker of the relata is washed repeatedly.

Exemplification Relation (cf. **Property: Monadic Property** above): the unique relation of a property or accident to its supporting substance. 'Being exemplified by' is an intimate relation that, unlike relations between primary substances (see **Substance** below), does not obtain between independent relata: hardness is exemplified by this table, but it is a mistake to think of that relation as a relation between two independent things, hardness and this table. For this reason, among others, some philosophers think it best to view exemplification is something less than a real relation. 'Exemplifies' is a synonym for the copula 'is' in all but formal and material identity statements, existential statements, and definitions (see **Predicable** above).

Part-Whole Relation (cf. **Relation: Exemplification Relation** and **Proper Part** above): the relation of something to a complex object by which it contributes to the constitution of that object. This relation, or course, is the inverse of the **whole-part** relation: the relation of a complex object to one of its constituents. The part-whole relation (and the whole-part relation) differs from the exemplification relation regarding, to cite one example, *dependence:* Substances exist independently of the properties they exemplify, and properties exist dependently on the substances that support them;[17] on the other hand, complex objects exist dependently on their constituents, and vice versa.[18]

Participation Relation (cf. **Universal** below): Plato's notion of the relation between, for example, a property and the universal it is an instance of. 'Having a share of' or 'participating in' a universal are how things repeated in the world are able to so repeat *insofar as they are the same*. How things repeated in the world are able to so repeat *insofar as they are numerically different* is the question of individuation (see **Individuation** above).

Substance (cf. **Matter** above): in Aristotelian metaphysics this term names the ontological status of *individuals* with a certain sort of existence. Since it is hard to give a definition of a category or ultimate genus, philosophers usually define substance negatively as something that exists *not present in something else* (like a color or shape) and *not abstractly* (like 'animal' or 'human'). *Primary substance* terms, like those referring to individual humans, Tom or Jane, or to individual horses, Trigger or Mr. Ed, are marked by the fact that they cannot be predicated of anything (cf. **Predicable: Predication** above). *Secondary substance* terms—like 'animal' and 'human'—are those classificatory names, genus and species terms, that in some sense refer ultimately to individuals (primary substances), though indeterminately.

Taking metaphysical clues from grammar, Aristotle says that a primary substance term is never *said of* a grammatical subject, nor is it ever *present in* a subject: *said of* a subject, as 'man' and 'animal' are said of Socrates; *present in* a subject, as 'white' and 'dense' are present in him. Everything other than primary substances, in the categories, is either said of or present in a subject that is a primary substance.

Substantial Form (see **Form** above).

Supervenience (cf. **Second-Order Property** above): a kind of property exemplification characterized as the emergence of a property due to some combination or arrangement of underlying entities—either substances or other properties. Properties exemplified in this way are variously called *supervenient, emergent,* or *toti-resultant* properties. W.D. Ross suggests that we understand the existence of goodness, a moral property (he more accurately says 'quality'), as supervening on various states of affairs, combinations of properties that are not resultant themselves.[19] One might think of the existence of *moral badness* as supervening on, or emerging from, for example, the following complex of action and property: 'S trying to embarrass R' and 'R's embarrassment caused by S'. Ontological commitment to supervenience entails a bar to certain kinds of reductive explanation—for example, eliminative reduction (see **Reduction,** section 4.3).

Transcendental (see also **Transcendental Inference,** section 3.1.4): sometimes called a transcendental property, a transcendental is a predicate that can be applied in any of Aristotle's ten categories and therefore *transcends* the categories. A transcendental is in an even more general 'category' than any of the categories. Being, Good, It, and Unity are some of the transcendentals identified by Aristotle. While a substance, for example, Socrates, can be white, his relations cannot be—neither can his actions. White therefore is not a transcendental property—it is restricted to the category of substance for its *exemplification.* But Socrates can be good himself (a good substance), a good father (a relation), and a good speaker (an action).

Good is a transcendental because it can be predicated in any category. It transcends the categories in the sense that it is not confined for predication purposes to any one or any subset of them.

Universal (cf. **Particular** above): a *general* entity such as blueness, circularity, humanity, and so on. A great portion of metaphysics over the past 2,000 years or so has been devoted to an investigation of the nature of universals. Philosophers question whether the names 'blueness', 'circularity', and so on, name *real* entities in some sense. They also wonder if universals are required to explain (supposing an explanation is required)[20] how it is that two or more things can be one thing. For example, how Socrates and Plato can both be *human,* or how this sweater and that book can both be *gray.* Consider an illustration. Here are two circles:

It is not the curve of the ink making the circle on the left sort of circular that makes the circle on the right sort of circular, because that curve of the ink is on the left rather than on the right. And it is not the curve of the ink making the circle on the right sort of circular that makes the circle on the left sort of circular, because that curve of the ink is on the right rather than on the left. In virtue of what, then, are they *both* sort of circular? *Sort-of-circularity,* of course.[21]

And it is not the pigment, dye, or light waves making the circle on the left gray that makes the circle on the right gray, because that stuff is over on the left rather than over on the right. And it is not the pigment, dye, or light waves making the circle on the right gray that makes the circle on the left gray, because all that stuff is over on the right rather than over on the left. In virtue of what, then, are they *both* gray? *Grayness,* of course.

Now the question or problem of universals is just this: How is this all possible? How is it, for example, that we can properly predicate 'gray', a *singular* term, of a pair of things? *They* are gray; not they are *grays.* This problem seems odd, I think, because we are all so used to seeing *everything* in the world repeated so much (it seems to me *every* item of immediate experience is repeatable). The world can seem a pretty boring place because of universals. But this ought not to lull us into thinking there's anything very obvious about how this feature of reality is even possible.

The ancient philosophers called this problem the problem of the one and the many (e.g., what is the relation between grayness and gray things?). Medieval philosophers sought to understand the *reference* of Genus and Species terms (e.g., to what precisely does the term 'animal' refer?). Later philosophers, focusing attention away from such classification terms (seemingly to avoid added confusion about the nature of abstraction), call the problem the problem of 'the recurrence of a quality'.

Chapter 2

Assessing Claims

2.0 Introduction

This chapter should be read with the immediately following chapter on assessing inferences. Philosophers are interested in the truth of claims and therefore with the assessment of claims—with what makes them true (if they are true), with how likely they are to be true, and especially with what accounts for that likelihood. They are also concerned with the reliability of *inferences* from claims known or believed to be true to other claims the truth of which they wonder about—the topic of the next chapter.

My choice of focusing on these linguistic issues is to accommodate the current methodological tradition of much of academic philosophy, a method sometimes called "Linguistic Philosophy." Familiarity with that tradition's standards for assessing claims and inferences is required before

27

proceeding to chapter 4 on philosophical analysis (a sometimes formal but commonly informal type of inquiry in the
above linguistic tradition), and generally to proceed in the
second area of philosophy mentioned in the introduction,
the area of epistemology.

Traditionally, epistemology has been called "the theory
of knowledge"; the name itself comes from *episteme,*
Greek: "to know." But that name suggests that epistemologists are not concerned with mere beliefs or opinions, with
claims less than certain, or with the probability of a claim.[1]
Though epistemologists talk a good deal about knowledge,
they talk much more about *justification,* that is, about the
varieties of good reasons for believing something.

As mentioned in the introduction, stubborn questions
about reality naturally lead to epistemic questions, questions about the nature and limits of human knowledge.
Such questions are naturally divided into questions about
the nature of the knower (issues in the Philosophy of
Mind), and about the truth of claims and the reliability of
inferences (issues in Logic and Epistemology proper).

The philosopher Gustav Bergman thought of the theory
of knowledge as an effort to discover *the ontology of the
knowing situation,* that is, what entities compose an instance of knowledge (e.g., some mind, a true statement, and
a certain relation or relations between them). Apparently
Bergman was thinking of epistemology as an issue in, or a
branch of, the philosophy of mind. It is also apparent that
answering some epistemic questions, so understood, requires answers to metaphysical and ontological questions;
but answering metaphysical and ontological questions
seemingly requires certain epistemological answers. Such a

tug and pull is a paradigm of a common view of the nature of conceptual analysis, as we see in chapter 4 (see **Paradox of Analysis** in section 4.3). But investigating epistemology *qua* philosophy of mind, which would be a species of issues in metaphysics, is beyond the scope of this book—an excursion there will not help provide context for grasping the tools required for general progress in philosophy.

The other division of epistemology, however, that concerning truth and the reliability of inferences, is required for general progress in philosophy. Philosophers are profoundly aided in assessing individual assertions, arguments, theories, and so forth, by the ability to classify claims according to the *kinds* of claims they are instances of—to which they have already devoted a good deal of study. That aid is not merely the assurance that one has not misjudged, because of the complexity of an argument, the amount of confidence to place in a particular assertion or conclusion. There is also the practical psychological aid of being able to narrow the focus of one's concentration to what is *outside* the general character of those claims.

For simplicity's sake, I discuss the following kinds of claims, using only true claims as a foil. It should be obvious that any way in which the following *kinds* of claims may be true, they may also be false.

2.1 Necessary Truths

The correspondence theory of truth (see **Truth/Falsity** in section 2.3) says that a claim is true if and only if it corresponds to a fact (or state of affairs).[2] To take a famous example, the claim "snow is white" is true on this theory if and only if (in fact) snow is white. To say this in more detail, "snow is white" is true if and only if the entity referred to by the term 'snow' *has* the property referred to by the term 'white', and the having of the property is expressed by the relation referred to by the term 'is' (see **Relation: Exemplification** in section 1.4).

With that understanding of truth in mind, consider the following two claims: (1) a red rose is red, (2) the cat is on the mat. Both of these claims are true, let's suppose, but there is an important difference between them. The difference of interest here is that one claim is *necessarily* true and the other is only *contingently* true. A red rose cannot possibly fail to be red—the claim cannot possibly be false; the cat, however, might easily have been somewhere else, that claim might very well have been false.

Let's step back a moment and consider what one might apply such a distinction to. One might wonder about claims such as "God exists," "I exist," "I *know* that I exist," "I know that *you* exist," and "The Yankees will win the pennant." Are any of these claims necessarily true? Some have suggested that "God exists" is necessarily true, since God is by definition perfect and existence is a perfection. Are they right? If not, what is wrong with what they have suggested? Investigation into the nature of necessary and contingent truths is useful for assessing claims such as these.

With these two general kinds of claims in mind, one might wonder whether there are any species of each sort. That is, are there any varieties of necessary truths and contingent truths? Philosophers have offered a number of distinctions among such truths; common divisions of necessary and contingent truths are listed in the chart below.

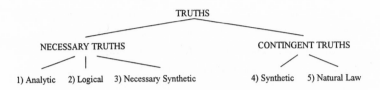

Numbers 1, 3, and 4 are terms provided for us by the German philosopher Immanuel Kant, number 2 is a common term from logic texts. Number 5 is thought by some to be properly listed as a variety of necessary truths, called *natural* or *nomological* necessities (see section 2.3).

2.1.1 Analytic Truths

An **analytic truth** is true because the predicate is *contained,* somehow, in the subject. Think of the necessity of the fact that anything that is completely inside a container is therefore, at least at the time, smaller than that container. Likewise, if a statement asserts nothing in addition to what is present in the meaning (concept, nature) of the subject, it is not going to say too much and thereby risk saying something false. For example, in the claim "a red rose is red" the predicate 'is red' says nothing beyond what is contained in the subject 'a red rose'. Further examples of analytic truths are: a triangle has three sides, 'liverwurst' has three syllables, and a red rose is a rose. Analytic truths are said to depend for their truth on their *content,* as opposed to their *form*—as do logical truths.

2.1.2 Logical Truths

A **logical truth** is true because of the meaning of the logical words that partly compose it, together with their *arrangement* in the statement. Here are what logicians call logical words: 'and', 'or', and 'not' (some think 'implies' or 'if . . . then'—see **Paradox of Material Implication** in section 3.4). These logical words are also called connectives. All logical truths then are *compound* claims in the sense that they are always composed of simple claims like "it is raining" and some or other of the logical words. For example, consider the claim:

Either it is raining *or* it is *not* raining.

This claim is true due to the meanings of 'or' and 'not' along with their particular placement in the claim. That placement amounts to the disjunction of a simple claim, "it is raining," and one negation of that simple claim "it is *not* the case that [it is raining]." Logic texts call these sorts of claims 'tautologies', logical claims true regardless of the truth values of their component statements. Notice in this example that it is also crucial that the simple claim remain the same throughout: "Either it is raining or it is not snowing" is not a necessary truth.

An important feature of logical truths is that they are *truth functionally complex.* This means simply that we can figure out (completely) the truth value of a logical truth (or logical falsehood, or logically contingent claim) by knowing the meanings of the logical words above, and the truth values of the component parts. The example above has the logical form 'P or not P'. From this we can see that whether P is true or false, the statement is true, indeed, *must* be true. 'P *and* not P' *must* be false.

But what of a statement like 'P and Q'? This claim will be *logically contingent* (it will turn out true sometimes and false other times): by knowing the meaning of 'and', and the truth values of the simple statements, we can figure out completely when a claim of that form is true or false. For example, take "Jack and Jill went up the hill." It's true only when *both* Jack went and Jill went. It is false when Jack went and Jill didn't, false when Jill went and Jack didn't, and false, especially, when neither of them went. Since those are all the possible combinations of truth conditions, the statement "Jack and Jill went up the hill" is truth functionally complex.

2.1.3 Necessary-Synthetic Truths

A **necessary-synthetic truth** is true because of the nature of the subject matter of the claim—both the referent of the subject term and of the predicate term(s), along with the relation(s) between them. Common examples of plausible candidates for being necessary-synthetic claims are the following:

a. 5 + 7 = 12 (or any mathematical truth).

b. If something is colored then it is spatially extended.

c. The angles of a triangle add up to 180°.

Let's make the subject-predicate form of the last example explicit for ease of consideration. All angles that are the angles of a triangle are angles that add up to 180°. The predicate seems to say *more* than what is contained in the meaning of the subject, and so the claim does not fit the description of an analytic claim. Still, the claim seems to be necessarily true, and so seems to require the category of necessary-synthetic truths.

2.2 Contingent Truths

It should be clear that the claims in sections 2.1.1 to 2.1.3 can be assessed without the aid of empirical confirmation—one need not "go and see" if the above sorts of claims are true. Consider our earlier examples: "a red rose is red" and "the cat is on the mat". The truth of the first is discoverable *a priori* while the latter is only assessable *a posteriori* (see section 5.6). Claims that require empirical confirmation to determine their truth value (truth or falsity) are contingent claims.

2.2.1 Synthetic Truths

One should not think, because of what was said above, that required empirical confirmation is what makes a contingent claim contingent. Contingent claims are contingent merely because what is asserted in the predicate is underdetermined by what is contained in or implied by the meaning of the subject—hence the need to seek out the subject, the reference of the subject term (the cat), and assess if the predicate applies (see if she is on the mat). Such claims are a **synthesis,** or putting together, of subject and predicate, rather than a breaking out of the predicate from the subject, as in analytic truths.

2.2.2 *Truths of Natural Law*

Like synthetic truths, **Truths of Natural Law** are the putting together of a subject term and a predicate term. The difference that makes the distinction between mere synthetic truths and the truths of natural law interesting is this: While no one will balk at the claim that the sentence "the cat is on the mat" is not necessarily true, some are anxious to balk at the common philosophical claim that statements of natural law, such as "H_2O boils at 212° Fahrenheit STP," are not necessarily true.

Defenders of such natural necessities admit that, in our example here, the concept of water is not *initially* rich enough for analysis to break out the predicate 'boils at 212° Fahrenheit STP' as an essential property (see **Property: Essential Property** in section 1.4). But why think that empirical confirmation cannot justify thinking that it is an essential property? Why not just include 'boils at 212° Fahrenheit STP' in the concept of water, making it a necessary truth? Then we can say, necessarily, and analytically, if this liquid does not boil at 212°, it is not water. We can build the causal properties of natural objects into their *natures* and thereby acquire a deductive science of nature. Worries about how to tell when the right definition of some natural object is in hand aside, where is the methodological fault in this?

We should quit this topic now, interesting as it is, and leave for philosophy of science teachers the task of explaining the issue further and assessing the arguments pro and con for thinking that there are natural necessities.

2.3 Essential Terms of Epistemology (Part 1)

Cognition: usually thought of as awareness relating to truth and falsity—the awareness or grasping of a *fact* or of some *state of affairs.* The root of the term, Latin: *Cognoscere,* means to become acquainted with, or to get to know.

Concept: (see **Conception** below).

Conception (cf. **Perception** below): the act, or result of the act, of grasping *what* something is without regard to its existence—in **precise abstraction** (see section 4.3) from grasping whether that thing is, whether that thing exists. St. Anselm's ontological argument for the existence of God can be understood as denying that this definition is correct regarding every concept. Without doing too much violence to his view, we can say that he believes that at least one concept, viz., the concept of God, *includes* existence. The questions whether concepts are, all of them, the result of acts of conception or conceptualization, or whether some concepts are presupposed as fundamental and limiting of what other concepts can be acquired, are issues in the philosophy of mind. Note that I have not tried to say what concepts *are.*[3]

Definition: the act, or result of the act, of determining something to be a certain way. This sort of determining can be either clarifying (see **Reportive** and **Real Definition** below) or creating (see **Ostensive** and **Stipulative Definition** below). Definitions are typically classified, as follows, as either definitions of things (**Real**) or definitions of words (**Verbal**):

Real Definition (see section 1.3).

Verbal Definition (cf. **real** definition in section 1.3): verbal definitions are the definitions of linguistic items, which may be either words or terms (terms differ from words in that they may contain multiple words yet only express a single idea, e.g., oak lumber). Ostensive, Reportive and Stipulative definitions are the most common kinds of verbal definitions philosophers discuss.

Ostensive Definition: the definition of something constituted by pointing at (with a finger or, perhaps, with a description of whereabouts, or by singling out in consciousness) the thing to be defined. "That color there" accompanied by the appropriate pointing at, say, the grass, ostensively defines green. Ostensive definitions are seemingly required to get the enterprise of definition off the ground. That is, definitions using terms must use terms that are understood. Terms that are understood are either understood in terms of other terms, or they are understood by pointing (in some way) to the thing that gives the term its meaning.

Ostensive definitions are also required to define *simple* things. Simple things do not have parts one might list to express their essence. The color blue, for example, has no parts (though blue *things* do), and cannot therefore be defined by listing parts and features the way one might define a triangle: three sided, closed-plane figure.

Reportive Definition: A reportive definition reports the ordinary meaning of a term—this is a dictionary definition. Reportive definitions provide the grounds for keeping people from insulating their views from criticism by making up languages of their own. We can say to them, and remind ourselves: "Say what you mean, or your words will mean it for you."

Stipulative Definition: A stipulative definition is a meaning assigned to a term for some purpose, without regard for how the term is used in common parlance. For example, "Mom, let's stipulatively define 'vase' as 'old piece of junk you don't care about'. . . Mom, I broke your old piece of junk you don't care about."

Extension (cf. **Signification** below): *that to which* a term refers or points to, or *the function* a term has of referring or pointing to something. Criteria for determining the extension of a term depend on the kind of term it is, such as a proper name, indexical, common noun, and so forth. The extension or reference of a term plays some part in the term's meaning—an issue in the philosophy of language.

Identity Statement (cf. **Identity** in section 1.4): There are two basic kinds of identity statements: formal and material. A formal identity statement is a statement of the form a = a, a rose is a rose, a cat is a cat. A material identity statement is a statement of the form a = b, the morning star is the evening star, Clark Kent is Superman.

While formal identity statements are *un*interesting, philosophers find material identity statements very interesting because it is important and surprisingly difficult within various theories of language and meaning to explain why they are not all obviously false, since they seem to say that two different things are the same thing. Gottlob Frege's answer to the question of how to understand them, to take an example, is to suggest that the terms 'evening star' and 'morning star' have the same *reference,* the planet Venus, but that each has a different *sense,* where the sense refers to the 'mode of presentation' of the planet.[4] (cf. **Signification** below).

Indexical: a term whose reference is determined by certain relations that obtain between the *use* of the expression and the *time, place,* or *agent* of the expression. That is, the meaning of an indexical changes depending on when or where it is used, or who uses it. This, I, we, that, now—are all indexicals.

Intension (see **Proposition: Intensional** below).

Intersective and Nonintersective Adjectives: these designations of adjectives arise from a geometrical expression of a distinction between adjectives and *pseudo adjectives,* and between adjectives and *relative adjectives.* If we think of the truth of the claim "the car is red" as expressed by an 'X' (meaning: there is something that is X) in the intersection of the class of things that are red and the class of things that are cars, we get the following:

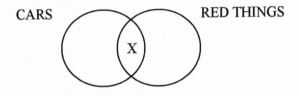

CARS   RED THINGS

X

The above then says: there is something that is both a car and is red. 'Red', then, is an *intersective* adjective since its being attributable to the car can be expressed as an *intersection* of the two classes. But consider an effort to express the truth of the claim "the mouse is large":

MICE   LARGE THINGS

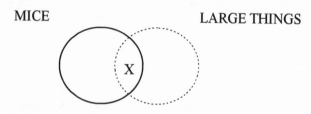

Clearly there is reason to balk at this expression of the claim. There is little doubt that there can be such a thing as a large mouse, but the expression above seems to suggest that that claim is properly thought of as the intersection of the class of mice and the class of 'large things'. And that seems wrong. I have used a circle with a broken line to represent hesitation at admitting such a class. 'Large' does not seem to be an intersective adjective; it does not name the class of large things because there is no such class. Instead, even though there is no class of large things *simpliciter* (see *Simpliciter,* chapter 5), there clearly is a class of things 'large-for-a-thing-of-such-and-such-a-kind'—and a term used to describe a member of such a class will be a *relative* adjective. (A *relative* adjective is an adjective whose adjectival meaning depends essentially on an implicit or explicit comparison.)

Similarly, there is a problem with trying to understand terms such as potential, possible, alleged, would-be, and so on, as real adjectives. A would-be assailant is not an assailant. An alleged thief is not, or might not be, a thief. A possible unicorn is not a unicorn. Expressed geometrically, "a unicorn is possible," though a true statement, looks bizarre if we think of 'possible' as an adjective:

UNICORNS   POSSIBLE THINGS

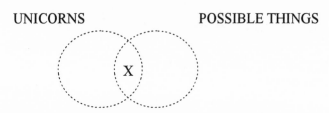

What does the class of 'possibles' contain? How much do possible physical objects weigh? How many possible things can we fit in a Campbell's soup can? "There are possible unicorns" should perhaps be understood as asserting: "It is possible that there were, are, or will be unicorns." Statements like "John is an alleged burglar" should perhaps be understood along the lines of this rendering: "Some are alleging that John is a burglar." In this way, we can avoid the impropriety of speaking of things as if they have properties that they seemingly do not have—when the reason they do not have them is, they do not exist.

Intuition (cf. **Proposition: Basic** below): the classic and least objectionable use of the term in philosophy is provided by G.E. Moore: "when I call . . . propositions 'Intuitions,' I mean merely to assert that they are incapable of proof; I imply nothing whatever as to the manner or origin of our cognition of them."[5] Some philosophers mean by intuition some special faculty of knowledge or belief. It is always a good idea, philosophically speaking, to ask what criteria allow the proponent of intuitions thus described to distinguish trustworthy intuitions from those that are not, and intuitions in general from other things that might be similar.

Modality: there are four modalities: Necessity, Actuality, Possibility, and Impossibility. The various species of all but the mode of actuality, which typically has none, are elaborated on in this section, below.

Necessity: there are four kinds of necessity commonly distinguished by philosophers (and these will mirror, as their complements, kinds of **impossibility**): natural, metaphysical, conceptual/linguistic, and logical. Let's consider each of them in turn:

Natural/Nomological Necessity: from Greek *nomos*, 'law', these terms name a very controversial sort of necessity that philosophers of science seek to evaluate—events that are, minimally, lawlike regularities—water boiling at 212° or freezing at 32°. Natural necessities have as their ground the laws of nature, or one might think of the 'laws of nature', as we identify them, as having their ground in natural necessities.

Metaphysical Necessity (c f. **Necessary-synthetic Truths** in section 2.1.3): any synthetically necessary truth would have as its ground a metaphysical necessity: something necessary due to the nature of reality. Metaphysical necessities are thought to be more binding than natural necessities, since it is easier to imagine different natural possibilities (water boiling at 211°) than to imagine different metaphysical possibilities.

Conceptual/Linguistic Necessity (cf. **Analytic Truths** in section 2.1.1): a truth whose predicate applies necessarily to the subject due to what is included in the concept of the subject or in the meaning of the subject, respectively.

Logical Necessity (see **Necessary Truths: Logical** in section 2.1.2).

Perception (cf. **Conception** above): the grasping of an external object "as the object it is." The qualification "as the object it is" is required to distinguish perception from misperception. Ordinary language suggests that 'perceive' is a **success** term. This means that the term implies a *successful* grasping of an object: to say "I perceive a tree but there is no tree present to me" is to misunderstand the meaning of 'perceive'. The various species of perceiving then will be success terms as well: seeing x, hearing x, tasting x, and smelling x all imply that x exists and that it exists as seen, heard, tasted, and smelled.

One useful way to think of perception, a way that is complementary to the scientific view of perception, is to view a paradigm case as composed of the application of a concept (a notion of what something is) to a sense datum (a simple or complex object of immediate sensory experience). On this view, at least part of what it is to perceive visually, say, a sail, is to have an immediate sensory experience of, say, white triangular sense data, and to apply the concept of a sail to it: the notion of something that catches wind and drives a ship. To misperceive a sail would be for any or all of the above components of an act of perceiving to fail.

Possibility: there are five sorts of possibility central to philosophical discussion: causal, conceptual/linguistic, epistemic, logical, and metaphysical. Let's consider them in turn:

Causal possibility (cf. **Necessity: Natural** above): a causal possibility is an event that would not violate any law of nature. The class of things causally possible is thought to be narrower than the class of metaphysically possible things. That is, reality might have had a different set of natural laws—water might have boiled at 211° Fahrenheit.

Conceptual/Linguistic Possibility (cf. **Analytic Truths** in section 2.1.1): a statement whose predicate might apply to the subject as a result of not being precluded by the concept of the subject or by the meaning of the subject, respectively.

Epistemic Possibility: this is a sort of possibility resulting from some limitation in what we know. For example, the claim that 'nine cubed is 723' is an epistemic possibility for anyone who has not performed the calculation when they're considering the claim. The claim happens to express a logical impossibility, it is *necessarily false,* which precludes it from being either metaphysically possible or logically possible. So to say it is possible that nine cubed is 723 is to say that *for all I know* it might be 723.

Logical Possibility: this is the broadest kind of possibility in that it is limited only by the **laws of logic** (see section 3.4). A statement expresses a logical possibility if it is not necessarily false. Typically, it is thought that anything that is conceivable is logically possible, and vice versa. And something is conceivable if it can be thought without *contradiction.*

Metaphysical Possibility: this is a sort of possibility due to the nature of reality. Everything that is *actual,* that exists or occurs, is possible in the metaphysical sense of the word; so, of course, is everything that is necessary. There is no standard test for determining whether something is metaphysically possible beyond that mentioned above (seeing if it is actual)—the test for logical possibility below is often considered too strong. That is, it supposes the class of things metaphysically possible is co-extensive with the class of things logically possible, which is to suppose our concepts are metaphysically accurate.

Predicable (see section 1.4).

Proposition: that which is expressed by an indicative or declarative statement and bears a truth value (truth or falsehood). The natural test for whether some sentence expresses a proposition (or for that matter, whether the sentence is declarative or indicative) is whether it would be natural to answer true or false on hearing it stated. "Close that door!" ... "True!" No, that's not right. "What time is it?" ... "False!" That isn't right either. "Bologna is grotesque." ... "True!" That's it. *There's* a proposition.

Beyond distinguishing kinds of sentences, indicative sentences from commands (imperatives) and questions (interrogatives), it is important to distinguish a proposition from the sentence that expresses it. The sentence "I love the girl" is obviously not identical to "Puellam amo"; nevertheless, both express the same proposition.

> **Attitude: Propositional Attitude:** any of the attitudes one has or can take toward a proposition. Doubting, fearing, hoping, believing, thinking it likely that, and so on, are all propositional attitudes.

> **Basic Proposition** (cf. **Justification: Inferential** in section 3.4): This term is used to specify a relation of a proposition to the knower of that proposition: if the proposition is known, but is not inferred from any other proposition(s), then it is basic. Commitment to the basicality of some propositions is an element in a Foundationalist epistemology—the basic propositions make up the foundations of knowledge and justification.

> **Intensional Proposition** (cf. *Salva Veritate* in section 5.6): a proposition is intensional (with an 's', not a 't') if the truth value of the whole is independent of the truth value of its part(s). For example, the claim "Eric believes that ales are better than lagers" is true or false independently of the truth or falsity of the simple claim that ales are better than lagers. Such claims are not **truth functionally complex** (see section 2.1.2 above).

Reportive Definition (see **Definition** above).

Self-Evident (cf. **Justification: Inferential Justification** in section 3.4 and **Proposition: Basic Proposition** above): ordinarily, these terms ('Self-evident' and 'Basic Proposition') are meant to indicate characteristics had by a state of affairs or proposition due to how it is, or is capable of being, cognized (see **Cognition** in section 2.3). A claim is **self-evident** if and only if it does not require the support of some other proposition for the one cognizing the claim to determine its truth value.

Signification: (cf. **Identity Statement** above): a term coined in the late Middle Ages, names the particular function of a term of *calling something to mind,* as opposed to the term's function of referring or merely pointing to something or other (see **Extension** above). The terms Superman and Clark Kent refer to the same individual, but they call to mind two very different things: a super humanoid alien in colorful tights and a nerdling newspaper wordsmith, respectively. Their signification is different, though their reference is the same.

Stipulative Definition (see **Definition** above).

Truth/Falsity: on the correspondence theory of truth (see section 2.1), truth and falsity are relational properties of propositions to facts or states of affairs in virtue of either corresponding or failing to correspond to the fact or state of affairs. On this theory, the statement "snow is white" is true if and only if snow is in fact white. Worries about this theory of truth might include such questions as: What is the nature of this correspondence? What of statements like

'There will be a sea battle tomorrow'? If the future does not exist (since it isn't here yet), is there a present fact about the future that makes that statement true? Or is there a future fact that exists as future that does so? Perhaps such statements cannot be true on the theory. If so, would that constitute a *reductio ad absurdum* of the theory?

Use/Mention: the distinction between two common uses of language that are sometimes confused. To *use* an expression is to employ it in its normative sense—to convey something other than the expression itself. To *mention* an expression, in contrast, is to call attention to the expression itself. For example, when I say, "Damn it," I curse; but when I say, "You know, 'Damn it' sounds cool," I do not.

3.1 Deductive Inferences

A deductive inference is a truth-guaranteeing inference.
That is, if the truth of one proposition guarantees the truth
of another, then one can make a deductive inference from
the one to the other.[3] The commonly cited species of deductive inferences are discussed below—along with mention of the relative confidence that has been established or
surmised for each kind.

3.1.1 Analytic

Consider an example:

A) Edgar ran across the yard. ————→ B) Edgar ran.

It is clear in this example that if A is *true,* B *must be
true*—our inference from A to B is deductive. Notice that
there is no need to know or believe or have any opinion
about the truth of A *at all* to tell that this inference is
deductive. One need merely see that IF A were true, B
would have to be true to see the deductive nature of the
logical relation between them.

As a species of deductive inference, we might call the
above inference an **analytic inference** in keeping with the
notion of analyticity from chapter 2: the truth of B is *contained in* the truth of A.

Note also that, in a sense, the claim "Edgar ran across
the yard" is a *less general* (more specific or particular)
claim than "Edgar ran"; here the characterization of deduction as always moving from the general to the particular is
misleading.

3.1.2 Logical and Categorical

There would of course be an analogous variety of inference to mirror logical truths from chapter 2, something I will call a **logical inference:**

C₁) Joe sits and Ed hums. ————➤ D₁) Joe sits. D₂) Ed hums.

Because of the meaning of the logical word 'and', if the compound statement C is true, then BOTH simple statements are true and we can infer deductively either (or both) of the simple statements.[4] Notice that the above inference(s) fits exactly the character of an analytic inference. There are, however, logical inferences that are not analytic:

C₂) Joe sits. ————➤ D₃) Joe sits or Ed Hums.

When philosophers refer to the *logical characteristics* of some theory or argument or explanation, they usually mean to limit attention to the deductive relations among the claims of that thesis—two claims are logically related if and only if the truth or falsity of one claim determines completely the truth or falsity of the other. They do not intend to include the evidence relations that might obtain among those claims—but they do intend to include analytic relations, if any, and also categorical relations.

Categorical inferences are those performed in accordance with the logical dictates of the concepts 'all, none, and some'. Consider the inference:

E) All crows are black. ————➤ F) Some crows are black.

It is because of the meaning of 'all x are so and so' that the proposition that 'some x are so and so' is true (so long as the statement 'x are so and so' is the same statement in both). It should be noted that this section is disanalogous to the section from chapter 2 in which 'categorical truths' do not appear. That is because there are no *claims* that are true (or false) merely because the meanings of the categorical terms they contain—though, as we see above, there are *inferences* that are correct merely because of the categorical terms the claims involved contain. For more on the logical relations among categorical propositions, see **Square of Contradiction** in section 3.4.

3.1.3 Necessary-synthetic

Necessary-synthetic claims also provide a basis for inferences. Consider the following **necessary-synthetic inference:**

G) I see a red spot.   ⟶   H) I see something spatially extended.

If there are such things as necessary-synthetic truths, and if the claim that all colored things are spatially extended things is one of them, that will allow us to infer H from G deductively.[5] Interest in arguments that depend on such inferences, as the one below, will all the more fuel our interest in exploring the possibility of necessary-synthetic claims.

3.1.4 Transcendental

A further sort of purportedly deductive inference has problems that also keep it from counting as a clear case of deduction. A **transcendentally deductive inference** is one that passes from the truth of something supposed or known to be true to another proposition, the truth of which is thought to be a **necessary condition** for its truth. The central notion of transcendence is that of *going beyond* or *transcending* some boundary. This type of inference was popularized as one of the main tools of Immanuel Kant's critical philosophy. He employed it to try to bridge the apparent limitation of human knowledge to the deliverances of sensory experience. Kant suggests that it is possible to discover the necessary conditions for the possibility of experience, and thereby to go beyond that once apparent limit. For example, sensory experience does not conduct us to any knowledge of our own existence as the subject of thoughts. Kant offered the following sort of inference:

I) Experience is unified. ————➤ J) A unifier of
experience exists.

Proposition J is transcendentally deduced from proposition I as a necessary condition of I's possibility.[6] I is known to be true if we merely notice that we can and do, for example, hear a sound and see an object at the same time. That experiential unity is possible only if there is some single unifying subject of the experience. Construed as a form of deduction, some philosophers, most notably Jean-Paul Sartre, have challenged the inference. Sartre rejects the deduction, arguing, by way of **phenomenological appeal** (see section 4.3), that the unity of the objects of experience is given in experience as *in* or *among* the objects, and not as provided by some single unifying subject of the experience.

Though the conditional, If I then J, can be supported by

analogical argument (see section 3.4), the analogous cases available are about things of an ontologically different sort. That is, the actions of bodies seemingly require that the body which is acting exist: if there is walking, there is some body that walks, if there is sweeping, there is some body that sweeps; but it is not clear, at least not to everyone, that that fact carries over to the realm of thinking or experiencing. See any standard logic text for an extended account of the criteria for assessing analogical arguments.

3.1.5 Completely Enumerative

A **completely enumerative** inference is, as the name suggests, based on having listed all the singular claims that might support a general claim as a conclusion. For example, consider the inference we might make when wandering along a car lot uttering the following:

> This car is red,
> K) This car is red,
> *This car is red (etc.)*
> L) Therefore, all the cars on the lot are red.

Said about cars on a lot, the above particular claims may seem to be deductively justificatory of the *general* conclusion that all the cars on the lot are red. In noticing that there are no other cars on the lot we see that our, say, ten claims and surveyance of the lot guarantee the general conclusion that all the cars are red. But, it seems that the *surveyance* of the lot, though a particular act of observing, is not a particular observation but a general one: "there are *no* more cars on the lot." The 'completely' part of 'completely enumerative' seems to require a general (universal) proposition in the premises for there to be a deductive inference based on those premises.

3.2 Inductive Inferences

An inductive inference is *not* a truth-guaranteeing inference; any inductive inference may be reasoning from what is true to what is false. Unlike deductive support that does not admit of degrees, the inductive support one proposition provides for another does: the support is either good, bad, or mediocre; our inference then will be either justified, unjustified, or whimsical. Within the philosophical literature the problem of the nature of the justification of inductive inference is often discussed under the topic of probability. Not all candidates for principles that would justify inductive inference are naturally classed as based on probability—causality, for example, might provide a basis for inferences that is not probabilistic.

It should also be noted that, unlike the principles of inferences discussed above, the following list includes *competing* principles (the principles discussed in sections 3.2.1 to 3.2.3): principles proffered as analyses of the same puzzling ground for *probabilistic* inductive inferences. A difficulty accompanying any discussion of theories of probability, which threatens to make the following account misleading, is that such theories are often at odds because of unsettled questions about the subject matter of the theory. Is probability concerned with an account of what makes an event probable, or of what makes a belief probably true? Or with something else still? Since I am interested in merely acquainting you with certain basic notions, I will not delve into details of theories of probability here. If you are interested in this topic, there are excellent discussions available.[7]

Here are the most common varieties of support philosophers have suggested as candidates for principles of inductive inferences:

3.2.1 Relative Frequency

A **Relative Frequency of Agreement** or **Statistical Correlation** between two propositions or, perhaps, between two events or states of affairs (or kinds of events or states of affairs) can seemingly support an inference. If one proposition is found to be true always or often with another, but it is conceivable that one might be true while the other is false, then an inference from the truth of one to the truth of the other is justified by statistical correlation. Another way of characterizing the same point, one that can help us see the requirement of *relevance* between the claims, is to put matters in terms of relative frequencies. To say that an event or proposition, call it p, is probable relative to certain conditions, call them C, is to say that given C, p occurs, or is true, more often than not. Consider the following inference one might make as a school kid walking home after soccer practice:

A) The lights are on. ⎯⎯⎯⎯➤ B) My family is home.

If A and B are correlated so that when A is true, B is more often true than not, A provides inductive support for B or, in other words, one can infer inductively by statistical correlation that B is true from the truth of A. Or we might say, and really should say to be accurate, that relative to conditions *only elliptically designated by A)*, which fleshed-out would include time of day, family habits, and so on, B) is probable if it is more frequently associated with those conditions than not. Such a view bases inductive inference on *empirical confirmation* (cf. *A Priori/A Posteriori* in section 5.6)—on collecting information about what actually happens. As we see immediately below, some philosophers reject the role of testing in determining probability.

3.2.2 Sui Generis *Making-Probable Relation*

Some philosophers, unhappy with relative frequency/statistical accounts of probability, which appear to them to have theoretical problems, such as precluding in theory a unique event from having a probability, have suggested that rather than events, probabilities hold between statements or propositions. Some have suggested that there seems to be a unique, or **kind-unto-itself making-probable** relation between certain claims, or between certain kinds of claims. This approach to probability then is offered in contrast to the empirical notion of probability—no testing is required in principle to ascertain the probability of various conclusions from various premises. For example, John Keynes suggests that nondeductive epistemic probability can be understood in terms of **internal relations** (see **Relation (Internal/External)** in section 1.4) that hold between statements.[8] In the same way that you can see that blue *is darker than* yellow, you can see that

C) Jamie drank seven   ———————➤   D) Jamie will have a
      martinis   headache tomorrow.

where the arrow is understood to mean '*makes probable that.*' We might then call this the *Keynesian* notion of probability: probability is determined by internal relations that hold among propositions. What is probable is the truth of a conclusion relative to various premises—not an outcome to various tests.

Ask yourself if the fact that you seem to see a tree makes it likely that there is a tree there even if we live in a world in which, unbeknown to us, an evil demon consistently deceives us with respect to the physical world. If the answer is yes, then we don't want to identify evidence making probable a conclusion with the frequency of getting things right. It should be noted that such an account threatens to sever the connection between something's being probable and something's being probably *true*—an unhappy result for the epistemological goal of finding inferential principles that guide us to truth.[9]

The *sui generis* making-probable relation is thought to be an irreducible (inexplicable) relation, and to be non-inferentially justified (see **Justification: Inferential Justification** in section 3.4). It is called *sui generis,* lit., of its own kind, to announce the suggestion that it is not eliminatively reducible (see **Reduction** in section 4.3).

3.2.3 Incomplete Enumeration

Incomplete Enumeration can support an inference. Suppose all that one knows, for example, is the following: The first car on the lot is red, the second car on the lot is red, the third car on the lot is red, and so on. In such a case, one will be justified by incomplete enumeration in concluding that the next, or the last, car on the lot is red. The inference:

E) All instances of kind *x* ⟶ F) the next of kind *x* will
have been S. be S.

is inductive but need not be justified by statistical correlation (in the sense that the enumerated premises provide support for the conclusion without being justified by being an instance of an established correlation). On the contrary, incompletely enumerative induction is often thought to be justified by the Uniformity of Nature Principle: "the future resembles the past." The difficulties with accepting this principle are, by now, well known. For example, David Hume objects that the principle that the future resembles the past is not an *a priori* truth, and can, itself, only be justified by induction: the future has resembled the past in the past, therefore what is now future will resemble the past. This, of course, is a viciously circular argument: it presupposes the truth of the very principle it is trying to establish.

3.2.4 Causal Relations/Lawful Regularities

Causal relations and **lawful regularities** can support an inference. For example, if one knows that it is established that heating water to 212° Fahrenheit causes it to boil, one can infer on causal grounds from G to H,

G) This water is heated ⟶ H) This water is
to 212°. boiling.

Causation can support an inference whether the inference is from a cause to its characteristic effect or from an effect to its characteristic cause. The latter reasoning is commonly called abductive inference—a variety of inference discussed below in section 3.3.

The term 'causal inference' can refer either to a *caused* inference or to a *free and deliberate* inference based on the assessment of a causal relation. We here focus on the latter, on causal relations awareness of which might epistemically justify us in inferring something. The former sort of causal inference is one that merely happens—the question of *whether one is epistemically justified* in inferring something need not arise. (To be reminded why causal inferences are not thought to be best classified as a species of deductive inference, see section 2.2.2 and **Cause** in section 1.4.)

3.3 Abductive Inferences

Sherlock Holmes is often said to be a master of *deduction,* a term Sir Arthur Conan Doyle suggests to describe Holmes's reasoning; but on the contrary, an inspection of his famous reasoning reveals characteristically abductive, not deductive, inferences. 'Abduction', a term coined by C.S. Pierce,[10] was just being identified at the time Doyle wrote his marvelous stories. It refers to what is otherwise known as 'reasoning to the best explanation.' Holmes chides his companion, Dr. Watson, regarding his general method as follows: "How often have I said to you that when you have eliminated the impossible, whatever remains, *however improbable,* must be the truth?"

Now the 'must' in the quotation suggests necessity, and

so the inference, if we take Holmes literally, is touted as a case of *completely enumerative deduction* (in our terms). Interpreted in that way, Holmes's claim is surely false: there is no *necessity* of a conclusion based on what is left over after the impossible is eliminated (unless every other explanation in the universe is impossible—something quite hard to establish). Consider an example of Holmes's reasoning from "The Science of Deduction" in *The Sign of Four*. Dr. Watson (narrating), in an attempt to humble Holmes, has asked him to identify the man who previously owned the watch Watson has just come to possess:

> "He was a man of untidy habits—very untidy and careless. He was left with good prospects, but he threw away his chances, lived for some time in poverty with occasional short intervals of prosperity, and finally, taking to drink, he died. That is all I can gather."
>
> I sprang from my chair and limped impatiently about the room with considerable bitterness in my heart. . . .
>
> "My dear doctor," he said kindly, "pray accept my apologies. Viewing the matter as an abstract problem, I had forgotten how personal and painful a thing it might be to you. I assure you, however, that I never even knew you had a brother until you handed me the watch."
>
> "Then how in the name of all that is wonderful did you get these facts? They are absolutely correct in every particular."
>
> "Ah, that is good luck. I could only say what was the balance of probability. I did not at all expect to be so accurate."
>
> "But it was not mere guesswork?"
>
> "No, no: I never guess. It is a shocking habit—destructive to the logical faculty. What seems strange to you is only so because you do not follow my train of thought or observe the small facts upon which large inferences may depend. For ex-

ample I began by stating that your brother was careless. When you observe the lower part of the watch-case you notice that it is not only dinted in two places but it is cut and marked all over from the habit of keeping other hard objects, such as coins or keys, in the same pocket. Surely it is no great feat to assume that a man who treats a fifty-guinea watch so cavalierly must be a careless man. Neither is it a very far-fetched inference that a man who inherits one article of such value is pretty well provided for in other respects."

I nodded to show that I followed his reasoning.

"It is very customary for pawnbrokers in England, when they take a watch, to scratch the numbers of the ticket with a pinpoint upon the inside of the case. It is more handy than a label as there is no risk of the number being lost or transposed. There are no less than four such numbers visible to my lens on the inside of this case. Inference—that your brother was often at low water. Secondary inference—that he had occasional bursts of prosperity, or he could not have redeemed the pledge. Finally, I ask you to look at the inner plate, which contains the keyhole. Look at the thousands of scratches all around the hole—marks where the key has slipped. What sober man's key could have scored those grooves? But you will never see a drunkard's watch without them. He winds it at night, and he leaves these traces of his unsteady hand. Where is the mystery in all this?"

What sorts of inferences can we identify in this piece? The inferences from the dinted and marked-up watch-case to the watch being kept in a pocket with coin and key, and from that to the owner being careless are by no means deductive. There is no *guarantee* in either case—no logical, conceptual, synthetic, or even natural necessity. The reasoning is from effects to causes, and since effects can have more than one cause, we might say that cause and effect are always *logically distinct*—the reasoning relies on inductive support. The four numbers scratched inside the case are thought to suggest repeated possession by a pawnbroker as the best explanation for their presence. Again there is no guarantee that the numbers were etched by a pawnbroker— it is possible, for example, that Watson put them there purposely to deceive Holmes. But since Watson is not known by Holmes to be aware of such a habit of pawnbrokers, Holmes seemingly does not think that explanation for their appearance is very likely—not the *best* explanation for their appearance.

Holmes's convictions about what best explains the observed data in this case rest on his awareness of certain regularities: the habits of those who might have possessed the watch. Awareness of such regularities is established, in the first instance, merely by observing people and noting what they do *regularly*. Enumerating instances of certain actions strengthens belief about what goals or ends people have; and knowing what ends people have gives one information about what means they will choose to attain those ends. For example, knowing that pawnbrokers must keep careful track of their inventory and that they often accomplish that by etching numbers inside their purchases gives one a *rule* to refer to in cases where there is no observation of the present case available. The method looks like this:

A) General Experience ———➤ B) General Rules (life observations)

C) General Rules and ———➤ D) Best Explanation
Current Observations
(scratches on watch)

A very observant person can reason great distances in this manner, as Doyle showed us in his stories. It is very difficult to accomplish the same sort of detective work if one is limited to deductive inferences alone, as should be obvious.

At this juncture, let's make a long-standing philosophical conundrum provide us with an exercise to test our understanding of the varieties both of claims and inferences we've been discussing.

ILLUSTRATION OF ASSESSING INFERENCES

Consider the inference:

A) I seem to see a tree. ————➤ B) I see a tree.

Deduction? It is a commonsense view of things that for most people who can see, they will occasionally see trees. But philosophers often say that, since an hallucination, a dream, or the diabolical experiment of a superscientist *could be* deceiving us on seemingly any particular occasion, it is clearly false that the claim "I see a tree" *must* be true whenever one is having the experience commonly called 'seeing a tree'. Hence, a philosopher should say, on having the experience of seemingly seeing a tree: "I seem to see a tree, *but I do not know that I see a tree.*"

In other words, regarding the question of perceptual knowledge, A is the proper starting point, and the truth of A does not guarantee the truth of B. To clarify, A does not guarantee the truth of B if B includes at least this much in its meaning: I see (where 'see' is a success term, see **Perception** in section 2.3) an object that exists independently of and external to my experiences of it (unlike a dream object or an hallucination). The inference from A to B is not deductive.

Induction? We might think that the truth of B is made probable somehow by the truth of A. Perhaps the inference can be supported by an inductive principle? But notice that the methods of inductive support for a claim minimally require that one establish or perceive an established correlation between one statement being true and another statement being true.[11] Now, though we can seem to see a tree as many times as we like (i.e., we can have the experience of 'being appeared to treely' as *adverbial* theorists have suggested we label the experience of 'seeing a tree'),[12] how do we establish that there is a tree present when it seems to us that we are seeing one? That is, how do we establish such a correlation?

Perhaps we will ask others if there is in fact a tree present when it seems to us that there is. But that surely will not help matters: other people have the same perceptual status as the tree we are after, and so may be dream objects or hallucinations as well.

Perhaps we will grab the tree and scuff our hands rubbing the bark to establish its existence outside our minds. But again, that is all dreamed or we are the playthings of a superscientist on a distant planet. We cannot seem to push aside our experiences to see a reality external to them; we cannot seem to get a peek around the deliverances of our senses (if that is what our experiences are directly of), to see the world that exists apart from them.

Abduction? We might think that the existence of a tree external to us is the best explanation for our seeming to see a tree, and here we shall find a trustworthy variety of inference that will bring back our confidence that we do have good epistemic reason to believe we see trees on occasion.

But abduction is built upon, presupposes, induction of some sort discussed above in section 3.2. Instances of a justifying relation need to be counted, it would seem, by counting the times the relata occur together. We can add up the A's, but we seemingly can never be sure of *any* B's. Abduction seems to fail to extricate us from this classic philosophical problem as well.

Showing how we do in fact possess *perceptual knowledge,* knowledge of an externally existing physical world, has been a surprisingly difficult and frustrating endeavor ever since the challenging presentation of the problem by René Descartes around 1640.[13] Under the course title "History of Modern Philosophy" one can discover the details of this interesting topic.

3.4 Essential Terms of Epistemology (Part 2)

Analogical Reasoning/Argument: a kind of inductive reasoning or argument that points out that two or more things are analogous in certain respects and therefore can be expected to be analogous in the respect under consideration. "This toy will probably break" can be supported by analogical argument by citing another toy, made by the same company, at the same factory, by the same workers, in the same year, and so on, that broke.

Bracketing (cf. **Definition: Stipulative** in section 2.3, **Presupposition** and **Dialectical Argument/Reasoning** below): marking off an issue or set of issues from other relevant considerations for some given purpose. Or, excluding certain elements of a concept to obtain a subject matter free of that concept's ordinary commitments.

Conditional Statement: a compound statement of the form "If P then Q." The statement, either simple or compound, that P stands for is called the antecedent, and the statement, either simple or compound, that Q stands for is called the consequent. The conditional statement, taken as a whole, asserts that a relation holds between the antecedent and the consequent such that P is a sufficient (but not necessary) condition for Q and Q is a necessary (but not sufficient) condition for P (see **Sufficient Condition** and **Necessary Condition** below).

> **Subjunctive Conditionals:** 'If, then' statements in the subjunctive mood (were/would) that are either counterfactual or hypothetical. In philosophy, such statements are often used to express suggested analyses of the meaning of dispositional properties. For example, "x is fragile" can be analyzed, in part, as meaning "If one were to hit object x with a hammer, x would shatter." Or such statements are used to express suggested analyses of statements of natural law: Water boils under standard temperature and pressure at 212° Fahrenheit means "If one were to raise the temperature of some quantity of water under STP to 212° Fahrenheit, then that water would boil."

Demonstration (cf. **Dialectical Argument** below): a proof that does not require supposition. A demonstration proceeds from premises that are known to be true to a conclusion(s) that follows deductively, that is, via inference rules that are known to be truth preserving. Demonstrations are the strictest sort of proof. Aristotle, who develops this notion of demonstration in his *Prior Analytics* and *Posterior Analytics,* suggests the following criteria for premises of a demonstration:

1. True
2. Primary
3. Immediate
4. Better known than conclusion
5. Prior (logically) to the conclusion
6. Related to conclusion as cause to effect

Dialectical Argument/Reasoning: (cf. **Demonstration** above): a proof or line of inference that relies on premises that are not known to be true but are supposed in order to show what follows from them if they are in fact true.

Discursive Reasoning: reasoning bound together by relevance. Nondiscursive reason occurs when there is a break in the chain of relevance of premises to conclusions. For example: (1) If the soul is simple, then it has no parts; (2) if the soul has no parts, then it cannot be destroyed by coming apart; (3) if the soul cannot be destroyed by coming apart, then the soul is immortal; (4) if the soul is immortal, then I'll never need to buy another pair of shoes.

The above chain of reasoning fails to be discursive

throughout because of a failure of relevance between the antecedent and the consequent of one of its four conditional statements.

Entailment: a term coined by the British philosopher G.E. Moore, entailment is the logical notion of one statement's truth guaranteeing the truth of another. In such cases the first statement's truth (or falsity) is said to entail the truth (or falsity) of the second.

Evidence: a term often used to name objects or testimony that support some claim. Something is evidence if and only if it functions as a support for the truth of some claim other than itself and does not entail or guarantee the truth of that other claim, in which case it ceases to be evidential and becomes demonstrative.

Evident (cf. **Self-Evident** in section 2.3): a claim is **evident** if and only if its truth value is determined in the light of some sufficient reason other than itself, either in the form of some other proposition(s) or some state(s) of affairs.

Implication: a directional relation that holds between propositions and provides grounds for an inference from one to the other.

> **Logical Implication:** Logicians call implication *logical* implication when the premises conditionally guarantee the conclusion due to the form of the argument alone, as in this case: Either A or B is true, B is not true, therefore, A is true (this argument form is called **Disjunctive Syl-**

logism). Which statements are substituted for A and B, true *or false, never* matters for whether the premises *logically* imply the conclusion because logical implication is defined conditionally: IF the premises are true, the conclusion must be true.

Material Implication (see **Paradox of Material Implication** below).

Justification: the epistemic reason for believing something. As the term might suggest to you, there is a close connection between epistemic justification and moral justification. In fact, some have suggested that the root meaning of epistemic justification is moral—one is justified in believing something if one cannot be *blamed* for so believing.

Inferential Justification: the concept of inferential justification is commonly employed to illustrate the central thesis of *Foundationalist Epistemology:* If one is not *noninferentially justified* (cf. **Proposition: Basic Proposition** in section 2.3) in believing something, then one will never be justified in believing *anything.*

The Principle of Inferential Justification for Demonstrative Knowledge (cf. **Demonstration** above):

To know **P** on the basis of **E**, *you must know that* **E** *and know that* **E** *entails* **P**.

Consider an example:

The shape before me ————▶ The shape before me is
is brown (**E**).   darker than pink (**P**).

71

"The shape before me is brown" (known noninferentially because I am directly aware of it) entails "The shape before me is darker than pink" (known inferentially by inferring it from something noninferentially known).

The Principle of Inferential Justification for Non-demonstrative Knowledge (Belief):

To be justified in believing P on the basis of E, you must be justified in believing E *and be justified in believing that E makes probable P.*

Consider an example:

The Martians are ⟶ The earth will be destroyed
going to bombard us tomorrow (P).
with nuclear weapons
tomorrow (E).

"The Martians are going to bombard us with nuclear weapons tomorrow" makes probable "The earth will be destroyed tomorrow." But one cannot be said to be justified in believing the latter proposition if one's belief in the former proposition is based on reading the entrails of birds and rolling dice. That is, "I looked at the entrails of birds and found myself believing that Martians are going to bombard us with nuclear weapons tomorrow" (E_1) is a proposition that one can be said to *know* (see **Intension** and **Self-Evident** in section 2.3), yet does not make probable E.

The reason for thinking that one needs noninferentially justified beliefs (beliefs that make up the *foundations* of justification) for there to be justified beliefs at all is that an *infinite regress of justification* will arise if all justification is inferential:

Why do you believe *P*?
I believe *P* based on *E.*
But why do you believe *E*?
I believe *E* based on *E₁.*
But again, why do you believe *E₁*?
I believe *E₁* based on *E₂.*
Why do you believe *E₂* then? Let me guess, you believe *E₂* based on *E₃*, don't you?
Yes.
Is there anything you believe that you will say is *not* based on some other belief?
No.
You are not justified in believing anything then.
I don't care.

Supposing one really does care, it will be a start if he or she can see the truth of some claim, all on its own (like "I observed the Martians preparing for an attack'—see **Self-Evident** in section 2.3). It will be a start in virtue of having nailed down one of the *two* requirements for being inferentially justified in believing something. It will *only* be a start in virtue of the additional need for a noninferentially justified belief *that some claim makes some other claim probable* (see *Sui Generis* **Making-Probable Relation** in section 3.2.2). So, among the foundations of inferential belief, there will have to be justified basic beliefs (noninferentially justified beliefs) *both* about some subject matter and about some inference(s).

This principle of inferential justification is controversial. A famous example suggested to cause hesitation at accepting the principle is that of the chicken-sexer. The chicken-sexer can almost infallibly judge the sex of baby chickens but apparently doesn't know how he or she does it. Some would ask: don't these people have knowledge or justified belief? Yet they won't satisfy the conditions for the principle of inferential justification. Also, the principle is *very* strong. Think of the problem of accounting for perception of the external world discussed above in section 3.3. If we don't have philosophically satisfying answers to the problem of perception, does that mean that no one is justified in believing anything about the external world? Do only philosophers have justified beliefs?

Laws of Logic (Laws of thought): Aristotle distinguishes three laws of logic that seem indispensably presupposed in any discourse that aims at truth.

1. The **Law of Noncontradiction** (or the Law of Contradiction as it is sometimes called) says that something cannot be both A and not-A at the same time and in the same respect. The qualifications "at the same time" and "in the same respect" are crucial to this law. Without the time condition one could, while standing by a light switch in a dark room, assert, "The law of noncontradiction is false, A and not-A can *both* be true. See here: it is dark in this room and [click] it is not dark in this room." Without the respect condition one could merely carry an owl into the room and again assert: "It is dark in this room and [hoisting the owl up and down] it is not dark in this room."

2. The **Law of Identity** says that A is A. Every assertion and every thing is identical with itself.

3. The **Law of Excluded Middle** says that either A or not-A must be true. There is no middle ground between a claim and its negation. This law must not be understood as asserting that every dilemma is a genuine one. It does not assert, for example, that the claim "your action was either moral or immoral" is necessarily true. It may be that your action was *non*moral (perhaps you scratched your elbow). What the law does assert is that every claim or its exact opposite is true: "either your action was moral or it was not moral."

Logical Relation (cf. **Evidence** above): two statements stand in a logical relation if and only if the truth or falsity of the one completely determines the truth or falsity of the other. Simple statements are not the only things that can stand in logical relations. Compound statements can also stand in logical relations, as well as a group of premises to a conclusion or conclusions or of one theory to another.

Necessary Condition: something without which something else cannot be. Necessary conditions divide into the various species of necessity discussed elsewhere in this book: causally necessary conditions will be conditions for, for example, some physical event or events; logically necessary conditions will be the strictest sort of conditions for the truth of some claim or claims; and so on.

Paradox: a condition in which two lines of seemingly good reasoning lead to mutually exclusive conclusions. Or, if a line of reasoning leads to a conclusion at variance with something that seems otherwise to be obviously true, this would also be a paradox. Many "paradoxes" are not really paradoxes in the above sense. For example, the **Paradox of Analysis** and **Material Implication** are not really paradoxes, but rather are quandaries, puzzles, or just problems.

Paradox of Material Implication (cf. **Paradox, Implication,** and **Conditional Statement** above): the paradox of material implication, or more accurately the *puzzlement* of material implication, arises when one notices that on the truth table interpretation of the 'If, then' connective (usually symbolized with a horseshoe, '⊃'), the antecedent can be false and, regardless of the truth value of the consequent, the conditional claim, taken as a whole, will still be *true*. This happens only because the conditional operator in P ⊃ Q, read "if P then Q," is *stipulatively defined* as being logically equivalent to ~ P v Q, read "either not-P or Q." It is given this stipulative meaning because conditional statements are not naturally truth functionally complex: it is not obvious what the truth of if P then Q is when the antecedent is false and the consequent is true: if I go to the store, then it will rain tomorrow

This stipulation makes sense for the logician for two main reasons: (1) many arguments in natural language contain conditional statements—and so the horseshoe is elegant and efficient for translating such statements into symbols. And (2) one can translate conditional statements as disjunctions without much harm: "If the soul is simple, then it might last forever" can be translated without much damage to its meaning into "Either the soul is not simple,

or it might last forever." Below, you can see that the latter
statement, symbolized on the right, has a certain truth table
output in the middle column, derived from the four possible
combinations of truth values of its component statements
~ P and Q. Notice then, that if the horseshoe is stipulatively defined as logically equivalent to such a disjunction,
the horseshoe looks puzzling. Conditional claims with false
antecedents turn out to be true. Worse, conditional claims
with both a false antecedent and a false consequent turn out
to be true.

P	⊃	Q		~P	v	Q
T	T	T		(F)T	T	T
T	F	F		(F)T	F	F
F	T	T		(T)F	T	T
F	T	F		(T)F	T	F

So, on this stipulated meaning of "If, then," the statement "If 2 + 2 = 5, then I am the president of the United
States" turns out to be true. This oddity does no harm in
logic because, as one might expect, there are no valid argument forms containing the horseshoe in which a true consequent can be derived from a false antecedent. The truth
table simply says that the *conditional claim* is true whenever the antecedent is false, *under the goofy stipulated
meaning of 'If, then'.*

Another thing that clarifies this 'paradox' is noticing that
conditional claims in ordinary speech are not truth functionally complex. That is, their truth value is not the prod-
uct of the truth values of their simple claims plus the
meaning of "If, then" (see **Logical Truths** in section 2.1.2).

"If you like beer, then it might snow tonight" in no way depends on the truth or falsity of "it might snow tonight" or on the truth or falsity of "you like beer."

Presupposition (cf. **Bracketing** above): something assumed to be true, intentionally or not, that is crucial for the truth or correctness of something else. In assessing inferences one must keep an eye on what assumptions the speaker or writer relies on for the truth of the proposition from which his or her inference begins, and on assumptions about the sort or sorts of inference present.

When explicitly announcing, or implicitly announcing, in obvious cases, what claims he or she is presupposing, a philosopher is engaged in *bracketing* the subject matter. All philosophy must bracket somewhat just to get off the ground; even if all that is presupposed is that there is some meaning in the language used. A casual glance at philosophical criticism will reveal that a very large portion of what goes on is an effort to uncover illicit bracketing or presupposition in a philosopher's views.

Principle (from Latin: *Principium,* beginning. cf. **Axiom** and **Theorem** in section 4.3): a principle is a general truth or rule of some subject matter that governs what counts as correct and incorrect within that subject matter. The principles of reasoning, for example, are truths or rules of reasoning that allow one to determine whether some instance of reasoning is correct or incorrect.

Proof (cf. **Demonstration, Dialectical Argument**, and **Logical Relation** above): people generally use the term 'proof' to mean the marshalling of premises in support of some claim, *in the context of trying to convince someone of something:* Where's the butter? In the fridge. Are you sure? (Proof:) I just *saw* it.

Nevertheless, I can imagine a logician complaining that she is not interested in convincing anyone, even a hypothetical person, of anything, and never has been, and for all that still loves 'proofs'. There is, then, the sense of proof in which all one is interested in is determining whether certain logical relations obtain among certain propositions—the question whether one is convinced by something need never arise. In formal reasoning, a proof typically consists of citing the inference rules that allow one to conclude something from something else. That sort of proof might be called a *second-order* (see **Property: Second-Order** in section 1.4) proof, since it is the proof of an argument, and arguments themselves fit the general notion of proof above.

Do proofs always prove? This question arises because we often hear people say that so and so gave a proof that such and such, and we are left wondering if those people mean to be saying that so and so *succeeded* in proving such and such, or if they just mean that so and so *provided an argument (perhaps good, perhaps bad)* that such and such. Well, in ordinary language we do not have the word misprove or misproof, suggesting that the term is not a success term like perceive (see **Perception** in section 2.3). This might partly be because proving something ordinarily requires convincing someone, so to misprove something would be to convince someone by mistake and into a mistake—and that is a weird idea. Was the mistake on the part of the prover or the audience that accepted the bad proof?

So, I suggest that it is best to view 'proof' as a term we have to ask about: Do you mean *succeeded* in proving, or what?

Self-Evident (see **Evidence** above).

Square of Contradiction: a device invented to illustrate the logical relations between four basic kinds of categorical propositions in Aristotelian logic:

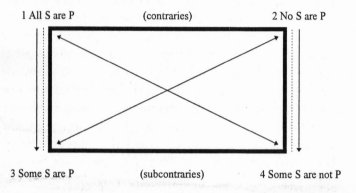

1 All S are P   (contraries)   2 No S are P

3 Some S are P   (subcontraries)   4 Some S are not P

The square is useful for helping one to remember the logical relations between these four kinds of claims. (And these four kinds of claims are useful because the premises of many arguments can be translated into them.) Here are the logical relations the square illustrates:

1. **Contrary**: two claims are contraries if they can both be false, but they cannot both be true. (Statements 1 and 2.)
2. **Subcontrary**: two claims are subcontraries if they can both true, but they cannot both be false. (Statements 3 and 4.)

3. **Contradictory**: two claims are contradictory if they cannot both be true and they cannot both be false. (Statements 1 and 4, and statements 2 and 3.)

4. **Subalternate**: two claims are subalternates if one of the pair entails the other, but the reverse does not hold. (Statements 1 and 3, and statements 2 and 4.)

Sufficient Condition: something which, if true, necessitates the truth of something else. Sufficient conditions divide into species along the same lines as necessary conditions: causally sufficient conditions are, for example, conditions that will produce some change in the physical world; logically sufficient conditions are conditions that guarantee the truth or falsity of some claim or set of claims; and so on.

Chapter 4

Philosophical Analysis

4.0 Introduction

Within academic philosophy there is no explicit canon of methodology for conducting investigation into a particular topic. This is good, of course, since the nature of learning and insight is not understood so well as to justify placing strict guidelines on how professionals should conduct their inquiries or guide their students. But there is a great body of philosophical history that has the earmarks of a rigorous discipline, and the Western tradition has an especially visible set of habits that constitute a method worthy of study in its own right.

4.1 Kinds of Analysis

In one sense, the kind of analysis a philosopher uses is dictated simply by the object of analysis, and so conceptual analysis is used for seeking understanding of concepts; linguistic analysis for understanding language and meaning; philosophical analysis, broadly, for clarifying or answering questions philosophers ask; and so on. It is possible, though, to identify kinds of analysis a bit more general than these by comparing examples of analysis.

4.1.1 Same- and New-Level Analysis

Taking conceptual or linguistic analysis as examples, we can suppose that in some cases what is analyzed will have for its *analysans* (see section 5.6) the *constituents* of those concepts or expressions; and since those constituents will themselves be the same kinds of things as those complexes they constitute, such analysis is called **same-level** analysis. That is, the analysis may be into things that are on the same ontological level as that which is analyzed. But it may happen that an analysis will discover ontological *reliance* on some other level or kind of existence. Or perhaps an analysis will discover *truth conditions* for some claim being analyzed, in which case, the analysis will be to a new *logical* level. Philosophical analysis is characterized by often being a *reduction* (see section 4.3) into, or an explication in terms of, what are *more ultimate* constituents or conditions— something called new-level, or directional analysis.

Take a statement suggested by John Passmore such as "England declared war on France."[1] Passmore suggests that, although such a sentence is in one sense perfectly adequate, in another sense it is unclear. The terms 'England' and 'France' are mysterious in the statement because their reference is not immediately clear (at least in the context of understanding how the reference of the term 'England' can 'declare war'). Analysis of such a statement will either seek to clarify the reference of the proper nouns by ontological reduction or by discovering statements the truth of which are presupposed by the claim, or both.

4.2 Tools of Analysis

In a sense, all of the tools, the terms explained in this book, can be thought of as tools of analysis (as well as other kinds of investigation). They are useful for breaking apart language, experience, and so on, into more manageable and less mysterious things. Many of the terms considered throughout this book, though, are *products* of analysis, suggesting that there are certain fundamental or basic tools that are not the products of analysis but are presupposed as analytic tools. I do not try to determine which tools are basic in this way, but that should not stop the reader from trying.

Because of the value of the present section for learning how to *do* philosophy, I take a challenging example of same-level conceptual analysis, from ethical philosophy, and ask the interested reader to take time for reflection on the details, looking hard at how the tools are applied throughout this long illustration.

A concept that will pay us well as a foil under analysis is the concept of *morally right action,* or 'right action' for short. At the same time we will be seeking, in accord with the first chapter's depiction of philosophical understanding, a definition (a *real* definition) of morally right action.[2] Let's proceed, then, and try to see both what clarification can be found of that notion, paying special attention to the tools and how they allow us to see the concept more clearly. Consider the following sections (4.2.1–4.2.4) illustrations of philosophical analysis.

4.2.1 *The Negative Way*

As a practical presupposition I will assume that all of us have a good if somewhat vague concept of right action already as a starting point. The evidence that this is a justified presupposition is the fact that everyone will be able to distinguish an example of right action from an example of, not just one other thing in the universe, a dog or cat, or mountaintop, but from other actions, and actions that are *not* morally right. Hence, by looking around at actions people perform that are *never* called, and so apparently are not, right actions (e.g., scratching their elbow), we can make headway using the **negative way.** We ask ourselves: What is it that strikes us about scratching an elbow that leads us to think it is *not* a case of right action? Well, we might say, it doesn't seem to *matter* if someone scratches their elbow. And people seemingly never say that someone did the right thing if there was nothing at all important about what they did.

So the first step of our analysis has the result that we think, at least as a revisable starting point, that *importance* be included in or somehow attend our understanding of 'right action'. If our first step or assumption leads us to consequences we think are mistaken somehow, we can come back and scrutinize our beginning.

4.2.2 Abstraction and Precision

So far it seems the *important* actions people perform are candidates for being morally right actions. Let's take a clue from ordinary language and see how the term 'right' is used in moral contexts. Sometimes it happens that when someone returns a lost purse full of money, people say that they have done what is right. Or again, when someone keeps a promise to feed a neighbor's pets, and does so timely, that is called right. If we subject these situations to abstraction, we see that what we think is important about them is that the return of the purse or the keeping of the promise has *consequences* we think are important. If we abstract precisely the action of returning the purse from its ordinary consequences of pleasing the one who lost it, restoring their financial condition, or others like these (or of *ever* having important consequences), we no longer see the value in it. That is, we think it is important that people do not suffer financial hardship and that a neighbor's pets do not suffer from hunger.

4.2.3 Distinction and Principled Distinction

It might appear, then, that we have found a satisfying account of right action as an action that has important consequences. But, to avoid a simple mistake, we can distinguish *by principle*—according to a fundamental ethical principle that good is better than bad—and add the requirement that the consequences be *positive,* for there are obviously important consequences of actions that are clearly not constitutive of *right* actions: all the destructive and harmful consequences of actions are important in the sense we have been using, but it matters rather that they do *not* occur. In fact, it seems pretty clear that those negative consequences will form some part of our understanding of morally *wrong* action. Furthermore, out of the alternative actions open to us with positive important consequences, since we can also distinguish between good and best, we clearly think that the right action will be the one with the *best* consequences— consider saving a drowning baby instead of keeping a promise to meet a friend for lunch. Both have positive important consequences, but we think it would not be right to keep our promise if it meant passing up the baby. So our notion of right action now has grown fairly complex:

1. 'Right action' =df 'the action that, out of the alternatives open to one at a given time, has the most important (best) positive conse- quences.'[3]

To test whether we have the correct analysis we must try to imagine some case in which a person performs an action that has the best positive consequences of any action they might have performed, yet is clearly an action we think is not right. If we cannot find such a case, the analysis will stand (at least until someone thinks of one).

4.2.4 Thought-Experiments

Casting about for such a case is what philosophers call 'conducting *thought-experiments*'. Consider, then, the fol- lowing thought-experiment aimed at finding fault with our proposed definition:

Smythers, the insane gambler, places five bullets in a six-chambered revolver and hands it to his acquaintance, Curley, with the following proposition: "Give the chamber a spin or two and point it at the next person to come down the street," says Smythers, "then pull the trigger. If you're lucky and the gun does not fire, I'll deposit one million dollars in the Feed the Children charity. If it fires, then someone will die." Curley, hoping to benefit many needy children, points the gun at the neighborhood grocer passing by after a hard day of work and pulls the trigger. The gun does not fire; the grocer goes home unaware of her brush with death, and Smythers deposits a million dollars in the Feed the Children charity. Let's suppose there was no alternative action open to Curley that would have had better consequences than the act he did in fact perform.

Here we have a case of human action where the best positive consequences occurred, as our definition suggests, and yet we balk at supposing Curley has done the morally right thing. I suggest that we are inclined to think Curley has not done the right thing because his action *probably* would have had disastrous consequences (about an 80 percent chance!), and so we think he did not act morally.

We might try to revise our definition number 1 to accommodate this case as follows:

1'. 'Right action' =df 'the action that, of those actions open to one at a given time, will PROBABLY have the best positive consequences.'

Under 1' Curley's action will not count as a right action and we will preserve our earlier conviction that the notion of a right action has something to do with important positive consequences. We now see that the ACTUAL consequences of the action are *irrelevant* for determining whether the action was right.[4]

How do our earlier examples fare under 1'? That is, what are the probable consequences of returning the lost purse, or of feeding the neighbor's pets? I should think that those cases will cause no hesitation for us in our endorsement of 1', for surely the likely or probable consequences of either of those actions are positive and best.

Can 1' be improved? Can we think of a case where even the likely consequences of an action are the best available and yet the action is not morally right? Consider yet another thought-experiment:

> Smythers removes four bullets from the gun, leaving one bullet in, and offers it now to Gubler with the following proposition: "Give the revolver a spin or two and point the gun at the next person to come down the street and pull the trigger. If the gun fires, someone dies; if it does not fire, I will build a playground for underprivileged kids down the block." Gubler, as anxious to do good as Curley, points the gun at the back of a passing stranger and pulls the trigger. The results are the same as Curley's. Smythers builds a playground for needy children.

Now we have a case where the action performed PROBABLY would have the best positive consequences and still it does not seem that that action is morally right. I assume we think that Gubler has not done the morally right thing because he did not adjust the possible outcomes for the value of their occurring. That is, if we assign a number value to the badness of the gun firing, say -1,000, and multiply it by the chance of it occurring, 1 in 6, or, rounded, 20 percent, we get a value of -200. On the other hand, if we assign a number value to the goodness of the playground, say +100, and multiply it by the chance of it occurring, 5 in 6, or, rounded, 80 percent, we get a value of only +80.

Clearly the balance of values now indicates what was wrong with Gubler's action. Informed by adjusting the possible consequences for the probability of their occurring, the value of *accepting the offer* is -120. This is called *weighting* the possible outcomes in the light of their probability; and it is something we all ordinarily do each day. Should we go to the football stadium or watch the game on television? The stadium is more fun (has more positive value, amount x), but there is a chance of getting caught in traffic (negative value, amount y), etc., etc.

Now our definition looks even worse, but is more accurate:

1″. 'Right action' = df 'the action that, out of the alternative actions open to one at a given time, has the best VALUE-ADJUSTED-FOR-PROBABILITY POSSIBLE positive consequences.'[5]

So once we look to the possible consequences of an action and adjust their value according to the probability of their occurring we seem to have the sort of deliberation required for constituting an informed moral action.

1″ seems to suggest that we understand right action in terms of the action's consequences, albeit a very specific variety of consequences. We must remember, however, the notion of intersective and nonintersective adjectives from chapter 1 and draw another distinction here to avoid confusion. That is, the "best value-adjusted possible consequence" of an action is not a consequence of an action because "possible" is not a real adjective. What looks like a huge adjective is really a complex description of an *intention;* and so our initial view that the consequences of an action are the source of its value was mistaken. Now our account of right action, after a lengthy analysis, looks like this:

1′′′. 'Right action' =df 'the action that, out of the alternative actions open to one at a give time, one INTENDS because of the expectation that it will have the best value-adjusted-for-probability possible positive consequences.'

Though it would be easy to carry our analysis further, let's stop and reflect on our method. Note that there has been no *mechanical* method of conducting an analysis here; the terms this book includes are merely *resources* for our efforts at such things as analysis—a good memory is needed at nearly every turn, and imagination, especially, seems needed with thought-experiments.

4.3 Essential Terms of Philosophical Analysis

Abstraction: generally, the psychological act of lifting out of some complex a single feature or subgroup of features for consideration.

Common Abstraction (cf. **Abstraction: Simple** below): this sort of abstraction employs simple abstraction but adds the observation that two things share something in common—the house roof and the garage roof are both black.

Precise Abstraction (cf. **Abstraction: Simple** below): abstraction that includes the act of simple abstraction but adds the explicit negation or exclusion from consideration of other elements of a complex (also called **Prescinding**). For example, noticing the garage that is part of, connected to, a house and then positively excluding from consideration that garage's relation to the house altogether.

Thomas Aquinas, following Aristotle's lead in taking metaphysical clues from grammar, suggests that the reason some abstract nouns do not function as adjectives is that they stand for concepts resulting from precise abstraction. For example (and this is greatly oversimplifying Aquinas's view), we can say that Socrates *is human* because the concept 'human' is merely the result of common abstraction from individual humans; we cannot say, however, that Socrates *is humanity* because the concept 'humanity' is prescinded, or cut off, from individual humans altogether.[6]

Prescind (see **Precise Abstraction** above).

Simple Abstraction is the mere act of noticing a part or an aspect of something—lifting it out of the subject matter by attending to it as it is situated among other things. For example, noticing the garage that is part of, connected to, a house.

Axiom and Axiomatization (cf. **Theorem** below and **Principle** in section 3.4): axioms are first principles of a theory—the most fundamental suppositions. The process of identifying the exhaustive list of such axioms is the axiomatization of a theory or system in a given discipline. Axioms may or may not be basic propositions—the axiomatization of knowledge would be composed of basic propositions if that theory of knowledge were foundationalist (see **Basic Proposition** in section 2.3).

Conceivability/Inconceivability: these terms are often and usefully distinguished from imaginability and unimaginability. Something is conceivable if one can know plausible truths about it; something is imaginable if one can form some image or 'mental picture' of it.

It is, usually, much easier to conceive something than it is to imagine something. Here is a commonly used illustration of the difference: Imagine a 1,000–sided figure. Now imagine next to it a figure with 1,001 sides. Now switch them back and forth really fast. Which is which? While imagination is thus shown to be a weak psychological faculty, conception is not constrained by its limits. There is little chance that any of us can succeed in imagining a 1,000–sided figure, but if you understood the experiment, you succeeded in conceiving of one.

Counterexample/Counterinstance: counterexamples refute principles; counterinstances refute generalizations. Suppose someone claims that all crows are black. That claim is equivalent to saying that all instances of the species crow are black instances. One need merely produce a crow of another color, a counterinstance, to refute the generalization.

Thought-experiments are the most common means of providing counterexamples in philosophy, since the discipline rarely has cause to make assertions about contingent empirical matters.

Isolation Test: the use of precise abstraction (see **Abstraction** above) to isolate an entity for consideration. G.E. Moore made the 'isolation test' a famous and controversial *a priori* tool for determining whether something has intrinsic value. If you are wondering whether some item has intrinsic value, compare in thought one universe completely empty, devoid of all things, to another universe identical to the first but with the addition of the item in question. Which universe is better? If your answer is 'neither', then your judgment is that the item in question lacks intrinsic value. If, on the other hand, your answer is 'the second', your judgment is that the item in question has intrinsic value.

Paradigm: a classic example. For example, torturing innocent children is a paradigm of morally wrong action.

Paradigm Change: a replacement of a fundamental thesis that implies a revision in the understanding of all that was built on that thesis. For example, Copernicus's heliocentric view of the solar system implied that astronomers revise their geocentric accounts of the movements of the heavenly bodies. In philosophy, Immanuel Kant's critical philosophy is said to have caused a 'Copernican Revolution' in that it seemingly implied that metaphysicians revise their view of reality to being limited by and to a great deal constituted by the nature of the observer.

Paradox of Analysis (see **Paradox** in section 3.4): like many uses of the term paradox, the paradox of analysis is more accurately described as the quandary or problem of analysis. The term 'paradox of analysis' typically refers to a problem of conceptual analysis: how do we know what concept we are analyzing, and, supposing we knew, how would we know when we had the correct analysis of it? For example, if we are to analyze the concept of justice, how will we be able to tell that it is *justice* we are analyzing rather than something else? And how do we know when we have found the correct analysis of justice if we do not already know what justice is in the first place?

For an example of conceptual analysis that pays some, but certainly not sufficient, heed to these concerns, see sections 4.2.1 to 4.2.4 above.

Phenomenon (plural: **Phenomena**): an object of immediate experience considered as such. Phenomena are the objects of ordinary experience conceptually bracketed (see **Bracketing** in section 3.4) so as to be considered the mere data of experience. For example, a flash of light may be to some a sign from heaven, to others a neurological anomaly, or to still others an observed physical event involving certain quanta of photons: all of this depending on one's conceptual or theoretical contributions to the 'flash of light' experience.

Phenomenological Appeal: a dialectical maneuver that appeals to the way things seem when one considers one's experience of something carefully. Moral philosophers often appeal to certain characteristics of perception to support their position about the reality of moral properties.

"Can't you just *see* the badness of an act of cruelty?" one might argue. Such an appeal is a phenomenological appeal.

Theorem (cf. **Axiom** above): fundamental, but not basic, propositions of a theory. Theorems are derived from axioms, or rely on the truth of axioms.

Reduction (Eliminative, Explanatory): the analysis of some concept, object, etc., into elements that are in some sense more fundamental than that which was analyzed. For example, an **eliminatively reductive ontological analysis** analyzes some object into elements that completely replace it and therefore the need to posit its existence (ontological status as existing). For example, the **purposive** nature of biological organs and systems might be eliminatively reduced into an account of the nature of causal 'feed-loop' systems such that one need not believe that biological organs and systems *have* purposes. Since biological organs and systems appear to have purposes, the above analysis would be **explanatory,** as well as ontologically eliminative, if the causal feed-loop systems provided an account or clarification of the purposive behavior of those organs and systems.

Chapter 5

Philosophical Writing

5.0 Introduction

This chapter reflects advice commonly given to philosophy students to help them avoid writing confused or confusing papers, and to ensure that they develop habits that lead to good philosophy. I hope these sections will be used not just as a strategy to write philosophy but also as a checklist to ease the natural anxiety of sitting down to write. Sometimes, a piece of philosophy so aggravates me that I have no writing anxiety at all. I sit down at the computer saying, "I am gonna squash this view like a *grape*." But other times, when I'm *forced* to write, for a class or a presentation or whatever, I get writer's block.

The standard understanding of writer's block is that it attacks us most often when we're perfectionists about writing: when we hesitate to put down a word for fear that it's the wrong word. Nonetheless, another form of writer's block seems to have more to do with a simple lack of direction. If you have a problem getting started, and don't think it's because you're afraid you'll say something dumb, reread this chapter, sit down, and give it another try.

5.1 Criticize, Understand, Then Write

A professor of mine used to say, "The fastest way to make a fool of yourself philosophically is to criticize views you don't understand." To me that meant every philosophical view there was. His advice didn't stop me, and I don't think it should stop you. Criticizing views you don't understand, as long as you are criticizing *in order to* understand, is one of the best ways to get ordinarily sedate philosophy professors animated and intent on straightening you out. And getting straightened out is, I submit, the proper goal of a philosophy education.

You may be gifted; you may be able to read Plato, understand him, and get straight to business writing a great philosophical treatise. The rest of us, though, may very well have to resort to the fool-making method to refine our understanding: "Is Plato nuts? Chairness is more real than a chair? Jeeez. Oh, picture this: Hey mom, I went to college and learned this chair isn't real! . . . Thanks, professor. Thanks a lot." In this way, in all probability, you will get a professor to defend Plato, and you may get something close to an explanation tailored to your own present understanding. Stupid-sounding views stop sounding stupid when the reasons for holding them are made clear. If things still sound stupid after a lecture, remind the professor that she has some explaining to do. As long as you do all this in the right spirit, you should succeed in getting the understanding you need prior to writing.

5.2 Be Negative at First

Another professor of mine held that it is actually good to *bore* your reader, in the beginning of a piece of philosophy, by taking the time to be explicit about what you are *not* going to be talking about. I am amazed at just how far into certain papers I can read without having a clue as to what's going on. Begin by saying something like this:

> In this paper, I will be arguing that a commonly dismissed part of St. Anselm's ontological argument for the existence of God is in fact correct. I will not be defending the entire argument. And I will not be engaged in a discussion of the history of arguments pro and con concerning his argument. Finally, I will not be examining Anselm's Latin text, so I will not be trying to say that Anselm's argument *really* is this or that—I'll just be arguing that given how certain others have dismissed a common view of Anselm's argument, they are wrong.

Though you will do well to begin a paper with the above sort of introduction, you should *not* try to write that part first, at least not in any great detail. Put down your main ideas first, revise them, write them again, revise, and so on. Once you have something you think sounds right, write your introduction and tell the reader what they are not about to read.

5.3 Identify Philosophical Commitments of Your View

This bit of writing advice is aimed mainly at students taking upper-level courses and those in graduate school. To ask those of you who are introductory students to identify philosophical commitments of your views is to get the cart before the horse (since it is to ask that you already know what you are learning). At the first opportunity at the advanced level, though, it is important to be mindful, in writing, of just what your view commits you to.

The standard way of approaching this is to announce what it is that you are supposing is true, that must be true, for your view to be true (see **Bracketing** in section 3.4). You can get into trouble if you do not see the implications of your own view. For example, if you are going to try to argue that 'Love thy neighbor' is the fundamental imperative in the correct ethical view, you are opening yourself to an easy criticism. Someone will say, 'What if I can't love my neighbor? What if I am so constituted that I just *hate* all of my neighbors, but I overcome that and act politely toward them? Am I then an unethical person?' Because free choice is a basic element in understanding moral advice (i.e., it doesn't make sense to praise or blame people for what happens outside their control), any moral theory suggesting principles of conduct must eschew those that tell us to do what we cannot do.

5.4 Distinguo!

There's a beautiful illustration of how to teach philosophy

now in use due to a happy new interest in medieval philosophy. The story goes that medieval school masters, understanding that philosophy is all about drawing distinctions and arguing, shouted out to their students "DISTINGUO!" when classroom disputations were hung up—and anyone who has taught philosophy knows that hang-ups occur often because of a lack of drawing distinctions. Sometimes it is just impossible, in the web of philosophical theory, to notice that two or more senses of a term are being used to different ends. An outsider, or we explicitly taking that perspective, can sometimes notice them.

In writing, this medieval practice translates naturally to the revision process. Help in getting things right is often found in looking for certain key terms that have a variety of senses, and distinguishing them. For example, modal terms like necessary, possible, impossible, and so on, should almost never appear without their philosophical qualifications: causally, logically, conceptually, and so on. (We can, of course, get too fussy about these things: I stand by my use of the term 'impossible' in the paragraph above.) See the explanation of the terms *a priori* and *a posteriori* in section 5.6 for an illustration of how distinctions aid in clarifying our ideas.

5.5 Using Latin and Terms of Specification

Because philosophers arrive at their subject matter through abstraction, precision, and the like, their assertions must be trimmed down to avoid referring to the complex objects of ordinary language. You can accomplish this with *specifying* terms. For example, 'insofar as', 'in as much as', and 'to the extent that' are common phrases available to limit the object of discussion to some aspect of what ordinary language is about. You will often see the Latin term '*qua*' (see below), in philosophical papers, doing the job of those phrases.

The Special Terms section below focuses on Latin terms commonly encountered in philosophical texts, especially in philosophical journals, along with illustrations of how some of them are used. Knowing them will help you read, and thereby write, philosophy. Some such terms you should use merely for emphasis: when the English equivalent is too clumsy or does not draw enough attention to the importance of the phrase. Often though, the term is conceptually rich, and will do for you in a brief space what a lengthy explanation might do.

5.6 Special Terms for Writing Philosophy

Ab Initio: lit., from the start. If you thought that some project was a completely mistaken endeavor, you might say that it was ill-conceived *ab initio.*

Ad Hoc: lit., for this. In philosophy, law, and other disciplines that argue, this term is often used to point out the dialectical cheat of introducing into an argument a claim that, though it aids in maintaining a point or position, has no justification other than it would, if true, aid that point or position. Often this term is used to refer to committees or groups created to undertake some special task(s) (e.g., an *ad hoc* board of inquiry).

Ad Infinitum: lit., on to infinity. This phrase is often used to announce that a regress of some sort is in the making. For example, a Foundationalist in epistemology might suggest that if there are no foundations to knowledge (see **Proposition: Basic** in section 2.3 and **Justification: Inferential Justification** in section 3.4), inferential justification will go on *ad infinitum,* and hence, will not ever amount to a satisfactory justification.

A Fortiori: lit., from the more forceful reason, cause, consideration, and so on. This term is used to point out that a particular reason *overdetermines* the claim in question relative to another reason. For example, if I say that someone could not climb the stairs at the back of the house, I may merely cite as a sufficient reason the fact that he or she is a paraplegic. But I may offer the *a fortiori* reason, the overdetermining reason, that there were no stairs around back to be climbed at all. And that goes beyond the former reason, being *more* than is needed to justify the claim that someone could not climb *them.*

Analysans/Analysandum: lit., the analyzing (the resulting analysis) and what was to be analyzed.

A Priori/A Posteriori: lit., from what is prior and from what is posterior. These terms are typically used to distinguish types of knowledge in virtue of their relation to *experience.* It is notoriously difficult to give a satisfactory definition of these terms, suggesting that the distinction is a poor one. Nevertheless, since these terms are very commonly encountered in philosophical texts, and useful in the right context, let's try to define them anyway.

It is often said that something in known *a priori* when it is known, or can be known, prior to experience. And that something is known *a posteriori* when it is known, or can be known, only after experience. For example:

A Red is a color (known *a priori*).
B The cat is on the mat (known *a posteriori*).

Because the term 'experience' is dreadfully vague, this account is inaccurate—surely nothing at all can be known prior to experience, since *knowing* is an experience itself.

We might improve things with two distinctions: (1) between sensory experience and any other kind of experience, and (2) between what is causally necessary for an instance of knowledge and what is evidentially necessary for an instance of knowledge. Now we can say that sensory experience is *causally* necessary for all instances of knowledge, but is not *evidentially* necessary for every instance of knowledge. Sensory experience is *causally* necessary for *A* and *B,* but it is only *evidentially* necessary for *B.*

So, the proposition 'Red is a color' is known *a priori* because, in coming to know that red is a color, a person does not have to go look at some red thing to see if it is a color. Red can be known to be a color *prior* to any sensory experience *one might seek in order to confirm or disconfirm the claim.* The proposition 'The cat is on the mat' is known, if known, *a posteriori* because, in coming to know that the cat is on the mat, a person *does* have to go look at the cat to see if she is on the mat. One needs a sensory experience in order to confirm or disconfirm that claim.

While the above account is somewhat clear, what should we make of these statements?

C John Kennedy was President (*a priori*? *a posteriori*?).
D I *seem* to see a tree (*a priori*? *a posteriori*?).

Is sensory experience needed to confirm *C* and *D* evidentially? Regarding *C,* we might say that because *C* concerns a matter of contingent fact, like *B* above, it is an instance of *a posteriori* knowledge. But unlike *B, C* does not fit neatly into our definition in terms of being confirmed or disconfirmed by sensory experience, since it is typically merely confirmed by memory—which is not a sensory experience.

Some have suggested that *a priori* knowledge is always knowledge of necessary truths (knowledge arising from reflection on the relations of ideas or concepts), and *a posteriori* knowledge is always knowledge of contingent truths (knowledge arising from sensory investigation into matters of contingent fact). This sits well with *C,* but what of *D*? Regarding *D,* we can say that *D* does not require sensory experience to confirm or disconfirm it, like *A* above, because it is merely a truth grasped by *reflection* on sensory experience (similar to the way one might reflect on "Red is a color"). On this view, *D* will be an instance of *a priori* knowledge. But still, *D* does not fit neatly into our above suggestion that *a priori* knowledge is always knowledge of necessary truths— since *D* is not necessarily true.

Despite these difficulties, the terms *a priori* and *a posteriori* have been and will continue to be used in philosophical literature. The context of their use usually clarifies what is meant and alleviates the fact that the distinction is, for the purpose of dividing reality at the joints, poor.

Ceteris Paribus: lit., other things being equal. A *ceteris paribus* clause is often used to do the same thing the phrase 'insofar as' does; but while 'insofar as' points to some feature of the thing being considered and excludes from consideration all other features of that thing, 'ceteris paribus' directs attention *outside* that thing to what one might weigh in an evaluation of it, and says pointedly: do not consider these.

Confer (cf.): lit., compare. Do not use this abbreviation to mean 'see' The idea is that one should look for a relation or relations between the ideas in question.

Definiens/Definiendum: lit., the defining (the resulting definition) and what was to be defined.

De Dicto/De Re (Necessity, Possibility or Impossibility): lit., Necessity, Possibility, or Impossibility from the meaning of the claim, or from the nature of the thing, respectively. These terms are used to specify the kind of modality under scrutiny or being employed in some claim. The truth that blue is darker than yellow is *de re* necessary because its necessity does not depend, merely, on the meaning of 'blue' and 'yellow' and 'darker than', but rather on the natures of those colors and that relation. Another way to think of the difference here is that the *de dicto* modality specifies conditions for the application of certain predicates to certain subjects *given the reportive use of language.* For example, statements such as "God is bad," "God is weak," and "God is confused," all express *de dicto* impossibilities because they violate the conditions for the application of predicates to 'God' as that term is used in ordinary language. Those claims express *de re* impossibilities only if God is *necessarily* good, powerful, and knowing—if he is contingently good, for example, it will not be a *de re* impossibility expressed in 'God is bad'.

De Re (Necessity, Possibility, or Impossibility): See *De Dicto/De Re* above.

Exempli Gratia (e.g.): lit., a typical or classic example, free for your pleasure or enrichment. Use 'e.g'. when you have an example for your reader, not when you are restating or clarifying something in other words (see *Id Est* below).

Ex Hypothesi: (cf. **Dialectical Argument/Reasoning** in section 3.4): lit., from, or out of, the hypothesis. This term is used to introduce a statement that is or follows from something *supposed* earlier—not always to the confirmation or disconfirmation of that hypothesis.

Explanans/Explanandum: lit., the explaining and the explained.

Id Est (i.e.): lit., that is. This abbreviation is used, in place of the English 'that is', usually when what follows it is short or requires special emphasis. It is up to the writer's good senses to determine when using the Latin is preferable to the English. And this reason might merely be that the writer has used 'that is'. previously in the sentence or paragraph and needs to avoid boring the reader.

Ipso Facto and *Eo Ipso:* lit., by the fact itself and for that purpose itself.

Mutatis Mutandis: lit., with changes for what changes. This term is used when someone, usually trying to illustrate a point using an analogy, wishes to claim that a given point can be made in regard to some subject matter other than the one in the illustration. For example, I may claim that a citizen is morally justified in interfering with the freedom of a big football player by stopping him from accosting a defenseless sandwich vendor. I may then claim that the same thing follows *mutatis mutandis* for the United States interfering with the Haitian government's treatment of its people. The changes would be from some citizen to the United States, from the football player to the Haitian government, and from the sandwich vendor to the Haitian people. If someone accepts the illustration but wishes to dispute the conclusion, they must cite differences between countries and individuals, for example, that render the analogy misleading.

Nolens Volens: lit., unwilling [or] willing. This phrase is used to emphasize the fact, or point out if unnoticed, that something is beyond someone's control. For example, often people consider one's beliefs so important they are inclined to issue praise or blame for what one believes. One might emphasize that, *nolens volens,* people believe what they believe—belief is not, at least directly, under our control.

Pari Passu: lit., with equal step. This phrase typically calls attention to the direct or inverse relations among processes, things, claims, and so on. If one thought that the rights of individuals or groups specify the duties of other individuals or groups, and vice versa, then one might say: "I will concentrate on identifying Smith's duties to Brown in this case; Brown's rights against Smith will become evident *pari passu.*"

Per Aliud and *Per Se:* lit., through another and through itself, respectively. These terms are used to specify the respect in which some cause has an effect or the means by which some thing has a feature. For example, physical objects might be said to have the *feature* of 'being perceptible' not through themselves (*per se*), but rather through another, such as light waves, sound waves, a nervous system, and so on. Similarly they might be said to *have an effect* on our vision *per aliud.* On the other hand, physical objects might be said to have an effect on light waves (e.g., bouncing them) *per se,* that is, without need of another but through themselves, or to have the feature of 'being dense' *per se.*

Per Contra/Sed Contra: lit., by the opposite side, and but on the other side. Medieval philosophical writing and disputation were often divided into a number of separate '*Questiones,*' or questions. These usually included a '*Sed Contra,*' often the citing of an authority, that divided the *pro* from the *con* arguments on that question.

Per Se (see *Per Aliud* above).

Prima Facie: lit., on the first appearance. As a dialectical tool, a *prima facie* claim is one that appears to be true, though perhaps is not well enough investigated or understood for one to suggest that the claim is plausible or reasonable. In moral philosophy the term has an important technical stipulated meaning regarding the nature of duty. W.D. Ross provided this use of the term to clarify the nature of duty: a *prima facie* duty is not merely an apparent duty, but something that would be an actual duty if only there were no other, more pressing *prima facie* duty that conflicted with it.

Though this definition is circular in that it uses the notion of *prima facie* duty to define *prima facie* duty, it does so in a somewhat transparent way that can easily be clarified: a *prima facie* duty is some action which, if there were no alternative action possible, other than refraining from the action, it would be a duty to perform it (and if it conflicts with another *prima facie* duty, it will be one's actual duty if it is more important that it be performed than that other *prima facie* duty). The clause 'other than refraining from the action' is important since it is apparently nonsensical to attribute 'duty' to an action that one cannot refrain from performing.

Qua: lit., 'as', or 'insofar as'. Aristotle calls metaphysics the study of being *qua* being.

Salva Propositione (cf. *Salva Veritate* below): lit., without a change of the proposition. This phrase usually appears in the context of testing the meanings of linguistic expressions. For example, the sentence 'I love the girl' is inter-substitutable *salva propositione* with '*Puellam amo*' (a Latin sentence that expresses the same proposition).

Salva Veritate (cf. *Salva Propositione* above): lit., without a change in the truth (truth value). This phrase usually appears in the context of testing the meanings of linguistic expressions.

Someone might argue that co-referential expressions (expressions that refer to the same thing) can be substituted for each other *salva veritate,* except in intensional contexts (see **Intension** in section 2.3). For example, since the expressions 'Superman' and 'Clark Kent' are co-referential, one can substitute one for the other in a statement without changing that statement's truth value: Superman is strong (true); Clark Kent is strong (true). But, in intensional contexts problems arise: Lois Lane believes Superman is strong (true); Lois Lane believes Clark Kent is strong (false).

Sans Phrase: lit., without the phrase or without the qualification. For example, a *prima facie* duty becomes a duty *sans phrase,* if that action's moral importance is not over-ridden by the moral importance of some action that conflicts with it.

Simpliciter: lit., simply. This term is mainly used to emphasize that something does or does not require qualification. For example, I may argue that things are not large or small *simpliciter,* but only large *compared to other things,* or small *compared to something else.*

Sui Generis (see section 3.2.2).

111

Videlicet (viz.): lit., namely. Prefer this abbreviation to 'i.e'. when you are *not* restating or clarifying something already in place: I am interested in doing something other than going shopping, viz., watching the football game (cf. I am interested in doing something other than going shopping, that is, I am not interested in going shopping).

Notes

Chapter 1. Categories, Classification, and Definition

1. There are other ways to conceptualize the world, but Aristotle's *Categories* takes its metaphysical clues from ordinary language and so naturally has been used throughout the history of philosophy to talk about the subject matter of metaphysics. Understanding the theory of the categories is useful because such understanding is presupposed in many philosophy courses and texts.

2. Plato, Aristotle's teacher, discusses the butcher who, as an expert of dissection, divides a chicken at the joints. That illustrates the point at hand: the world comes prearranged. The distinctions we make then should proceed according to the differences already present there.

3. Here is a handy mnemonic device: Kings Play Chess On Funny Green Squares.

4. For a number of interesting senses of 'definition', see Joseph S. Freedman, "Classification of Philosophy, the Sciences, and the Arts in Sixteenth- and Seventeenth-Century Europe," *Modern Schoolman* 72, no. 1 (1994): 37–65.

5. Many philosophers reject (for many and varied reasons) the conception of a substance as an entity *underlying* or *supporting* the qualities we perceive, preferring, for example, to think of a thing as merely a bundle of such qualities. Though it has been commonly supposed that Aristotle thought of substance as *underlying* properties, some think close scrutiny of his writings suggests a different view. See L. Susan Stebbing, "Concerning Substance," *Proceedings of the Aristotelian Society* (1931).

6. See, for example, Immanuel Kant's table of categories in *Critique of Pure Reason,* trans. Norman Kemp Smith (New York: St. Martin's Press, 1929), pp. 111–119.

7. Aristotle suggests two accounts of accidents in his *Topics* that are not equivalent. One is the above account: that an accident is something that one and the same thing can have or lack and remain that same thing. The other account is, of the things that might *belong* to a substance, if something is neither a genus, a property, nor a definition, then it is an accident. Why are these two accounts not equivalent? (See **Proprium** in section 1.4). For more on accidents, see *The Works of Aristotle,* vol. 1, translated under the editorship of Sir David Ross (Oxford, UK: Clarendon Press), pp. 102–103.

8. W.E. Johnson coined these terms and explained their use. See John Passmore, *A Hundred Years of Philosophy* (Harmondsworth, UK: Penguin Books, 1968), pp. 343–345.

9. I say *aspect* rather than *part* (see **Proper Part** in section 1.4) because the metaphysical tradition that treats of this notion holds that form and matter cannot exist separately (except perhaps by Divine aid).

10. See Anthony Kenny, *Aquinas* (New York: Oxford University Press, 1980), p. 44.

11. For a discussion of the possible explanations of what individuates, see Jorge Gracia's *Individuality: An Essay on the Foundations of Metaphysics* (Albany, NY: SUNY Press, 1988).

12. Kenny, *Aquinas,* pp. 38–49.

13. See Alexius Meinong, "The Theory of Objects," in *Classics of Analytic Metaphysics,* ed. Larry Lee Blackman (Lanham, MD: University Press of America, 1984), pp. 51–60.

14. See G.E. Moore, *Principia Ethica* (New York: Cambridge University Press, 1903), pp. 30–36.

15. For an excellent scholarly examination of these notions, see Hippocrates G. Apostle's translation of Aristotle in *Aristotle's Categories and Propositions* (Grinnell, IA: Peripatetic Press, 1980), pp. 54–60.

16. Roderick Chisholm recently employed the notions of compositive and divisive properties to argue for the simplicity and thereby immortality of the soul (mind). For a beautiful illustration of how conceptual devices can aid in answering philosophical questions, see his "On the Simplicity of the Soul," in *Philosophical Perspectives 5: Philosophy of Religion,* ed. James E. Tomberlin (Atascadero, CA: Ridgeview, 1991), pp. 167–181.

17. Unless, of course, the properties in question are essential properties. (See **Property: Essential Property** in section 1.4.)

18. This follows only, of course, if the principle 'the whole is (definitionally) the sum of its parts' is true.

19. See W.D. Ross, *The Right and the Good* (Indianapolis, IN: Hackett, 1988), pp. 104–105, 121–122.

20. See **Abductive Inference** in section 3.3 and **Transcendental Inference** in section 3.1.4.

21. I say "sort-of-circularity" because it is a commonplace among geometers, ancient and modern, that there are no perfect circles in physical reality. In fact, Plato, in his *Phaedo,* argues for the reality of Universals based on this sort of apparent fact. The idea is very crudely this, to keep with our example from geometry: we *know* what perfect circles are (geometry studies them), yet we have never and can never *see* any. There must then be Forms, or Ideas, that the mind grasps, and are the objects of such geometrical knowledge. Plato's Forms are commonly identified with Universals. For a scholarly and precise account of Plato's views on Forms, see Nicholas P. White's *Plato on Knowledge and Reality* (Indianapolis, IN: Hackett, 1976).

Chapter 2. Assessing Claims

1. Epistemologists often define knowledge as a belief with a high degree of justification.

2. The coherence theory of truth holds that the truth of a claim is constituted by its coherence or logical compatibility with other claims believed to be true. The pragmatic theory holds that a claim is true if it works, or suits our purposes in some theory or other enterprise. Both theories are commonly thought to meet with insuperable difficulties, and to confuse a mere test of truth for what constitutes it.

3. For a useful discussion of the ontological questions surrounding concepts, see P.L. Heath, *The Encyclopedia of Philosophy,* vol. 2, ed. Paul Edwards (New York: Macmillan and Free Press, 1967), pp. 177–180.

4. See Gottlob Frege, "On Sense and Meaning," in *Translations from the Philosophical Writings of Gottlob Frege,* ed. Peter Geach and Max Black; trans. Peter Geach (Cambridge. MA:Basil Blackwell, 1980).

5. G.E. Moore, *Principia Ethica* (New York: Cambridge University Press, 1903), preface.

Chapter 3. Assessing Inferences

1. See John Passmore's discussion of C.S. Peirce's logic in *A Hundred Years of Philosophy* (Harmondsworth, UK: Penguin Books, 1968), pp. 136–144.

2. Of course, an inference might be from a *group* of claims to another claim or claims, and so for implication. If you are having a hard time imagining a 'relation' between 'claims', think of an example: (a) I went to the store, (b) I went somewhere. A relation an epistemologist might be interested in here might be that (a) guarantees (b), but (b) doesn't guarantee (a). We can then say that (a) implies (b), but (b) doesn't imply (a).

3. Logicians call such inferences *valid* deductive inferences. Invalid deductive inferences are those *touted* as deductive, but are not.

4. There are much more complex deductive inferences based on the meanings of logical words and philosophy coursework largely devoted to teaching mechanical manipulation of those complexities: the enterprise of formal logic.

5. Although this is a classic example, and once seemed to me perfectly clear and correct, a philosopher at the University of Iowa, Tom Davey, pointed out to me that a minimal visible might be a counterinstance to the generalization "all colored things are spatially extended things." What is a minimal visible? To suit our generalization, a *red* minimal visible can be seen by putting a red dot on a piece of paper and slowly backing away from the paper until the dot disappears. Then, just when the dot disappears, move forward enough to get it back—*there* is a minimal visible.

Now, is that thing spatially extended or 'spread out in space?' We can't say, "Sure it's spread out; I just can't *see* its spread-outness"—we have, after all, defined our object of study as a minimal *visible*. Further, we can't say, "If I see it, it must be spread out," on the grounds that *anything seen* is spatially extended (we can't assume *that* since it is what we are questioning). These considerations should be enough to make us worry about this candidate for establishing the existence of necessary-synthetic truths.

6. J is a necessary condition of I's *metaphysical possibility*—not just I's actuality. The necessary conditions for I's actuality (causal possibility) might also include mere causal requirements (see **Possibility: Metaphysical** and **Causal** in section 2.3). And Kant appears to be after a stronger conclusion about the existence of the subject of thoughts, that is,

that its existence is required even for the metaphysical possibility of unified experience. Note that I —➤ J looks like a necessary-synthetic truth (with the added feature of transcending the bounds of sense experience).

7. See, for example, *The Encyclopedia of Philosophy,* vol. 5, ed. Paul Edwards (New York: Macmillan and Free Press, 1967), pp. 464–479.

8. See John Keynes, *A Treatise on Probability* (London: Macmillan, 1921).

9. For an excellent discussion of *sui generis* making-probable relations and the difficulties attending inductive inferences in general, see Richard Fumerton's *Metaepistemology and Skepticism* (Lanham, MD: Rowman & Littlefield, 1995).

10. See John Passmore, *A Hundred Years of Philosophy* (Harmondsworth, UK: Penguin Books, 1968), pp. 142–144.

11. Excepting the *Sui Generis Making-Probable* sort of inductive support, which explicitly denies the need to establish frequencies of getting things right for there to be good nondemonstrative epistemic reason for inferring something from something else. Nonetheless, solving this problem of perception, which is trying to establish *at least one* correlation between apparent sense experience and that which is the intended object of that experience, would require a very strong defense of such a principle.

12. Roderick Chisholm suggests this sort of locution for referring to *prima facie* perceptual experiences. Note that the claim 'I am appeared to treely' can be true whether one is dreaming, hallucinating, or under the control of some superscientist bent on deceiving people about their perceptual beliefs. Hence, an *adverbial theorist* has a way to retain a certain sort of perceptual knowledge: knowledge of certain elements of what is ordinarily called perception. Those elements are the same as the ordinary elements of perceptual experience, only they are divested (see **Bracketing** in section 3.4) of certain crucial features, for example: existing outside of and independently of the would-be perceiver.

13. See René Descartes, *Discourse on Method and Meditations,* trans. F.E. Sutcliffe (London: Penguin Books, 1968). In the *Meditations* Descartes provides his own interesting answer to this skeptical worry.

Chapter 4. Philosophical Analysis

1. See John Passmore, *A Hundred Years of Philosophy* (Harmondsworth, UK: Penguin Books, 1968), pp. 365–366.

2. Though we will be seeking a real definition, we will not be

seeking an answer to one crucially important question about morally right action: whether that concept applies to anything in reality. Answering that question would require a great deal of investigation into the metaphysics of morals.

3. The symbol '=df' should be read as 'equals by definition.'

4. Irrelevant, except, perhaps, in the sense that actual consequences are sometimes our best available evidence for whether an agent acted with well-intentioned deliberation and forethought.

5. For an articulation and defense of a version of this notion of 'value-adjusted possible consequentialism,' see Richard Fumerton, *Reason and Morality* (Ithaca, NY: Cornell University Press, 1990).

6. Or, more accurately, "prescinded, or cut off, *from the designated matter* (see **Matter** in section 1.4) *of* individual humans altogether." Common abstraction does not cut off reference to *any* features of individuals (though it does not refer to them all, except indeterminately, either), and so terms resulting from such abstraction can be predicated of individuals.

Index

119

Index

Cause *(continued)*
  formal, 11
  material, 11
Ceteris paribus, 106
Change, 14, 15
Claims, 53
Classics of Analytic Metaphysics, 114
Classification, 5, 113
  determinable/determinate, 12
  genus/species, 5, 7
Cognition, 36, 47
Cognoscere, 36. *See also* Cognition
Common, 14. *See also* Universal
Common abstraction. *See* Abstraction
Completely enumerative. *See* Inference,
  deductive
Compositive property. *See* Property
Compound statement, 32
Conceivability/inconceivability, 93
Concept, 36
Conception, 36, 43
Conceptual analysis. *See* Analysis
Conceptual/linguistic necessity. *See*
  Modality
Conceptual/linguistic possibility. *See*
  Modality
Conditional claim/statement, 68, 76, 77
Confer, 106
Conjunctive property. *See* Property
Consequence, 86
Constituent, 83
Content, 31
Contingent truths, 34
Continuant, 12
Contradiction, 45
Contradictory, 81
Contrary, 80
Conventional, xi
Counterexample/counterinstance, 93
Critique of Pure Reason, 114

De dicto, 106
De dicto/de re 106, 107
De re, 106, 107
Deduction, 61, 65
Deductive inference. *See* Inference

Definiens/Definiendum, 106
Defining, 8
Definition, 8, 36, 46, 47, 113
  real, 8, 36, 85
  verbal, 8, 36, 37
    ostensive, 36, 37
    reportive, 36, 37, 46, 106
    stipulative, 36, 38, 47, 68, 76
Demonstration, 69, 71, 78
Dependence, 22
Designated matter, 118
Determinable/determinate.
  See Classification
Dialectical argument/reasoning, 68,
  69, 78, 107
Difference, 8
Directedness, 14
Discourse on Method and Meditations,
  117
Discursive reasoning, 69
Disjunctive property. *See* Property
Disjunctive syllogism, 70, 71
Distinction and principled distinction,
  86
Distinguo, 100
Divisive property. *See* Property

Efficient cause. *See* Cause
Eliminatively reductive analysis. *See*
  Analysis
Emergence, 24
Empirical confirmation, 58
Encyclopedia of Philosophy, The,
  115, 117
Entailment, 70
Eo Ipso, 108
Episteme, 28
Epistemic possibility. *See* Modality
Epistemically justified, 61. *See also*
  Inferential justification
Epistemology, xvi, 28, 36, 67, 71
Essence, 9, 12
Essential property. *See* Property
Evidence, 70, 75, 80
Evident, 70
Evidentially, 104

Index

Index

Index

Index

124

About the Author

Steven Aspenson received his Ph.D. in medieval philosophy from the University of Iowa and his B.S. in biology and philosophy from the University of Wisconsin-LaCrosse. He has published articles on the philosophy of religion and medieval philosophy and is currently working on a book about happiness and a book about the Christian doctrine of atonement.